# MANAGING CIVIC AND
# COMMUNITY ENGAGEMENT

# MANAGING CIVIC AND COMMUNITY ENGAGEMENT

## David Watson

Open University Press

Open University Press
McGraw-Hill Education
McGraw-Hill House
Shoppenhangers Road
Maidenhead
Berkshire
England
SL6 2QL

email: enquiries@openup.co.uk
world wide web: www.openup.co.uk

and Two Penn Plaza, New York, NY 10121–2289, USA


First published 2007

A catalogue record of this book is available from the British Library

ISBN-13: 978 0 335 22046 5 (pb) 978 0 335 22047 2 (hb)
ISBN-10: 0 335 22046 0 (pb) 0 335 22047 9 (hb)


Library of Congress Cataloguing-in-Publication Data
CIP data applied for

Typeset by YHT Ltd, London
Printed in the UK by Bell & Bain Ltd, Glasgow

The *McGraw-Hill* Companies

For Ron Dearing

# CONTENTS

# LIST OF FIGURES

# LIST OF TABLES

# FOREWORD

Universities are vital to the health of nations, of regions, and of communities; never more so than in the context of today's global knowledge economy, with all its strains and imperfections as well as its dynamism and opportunities. In my 2003 review of Business–University Collaboration, I attempted to take stock of one particularly important set of relationships (Lambert 2003). The synergy between business, industry and higher education is one that all the parties, and the government, need to work on and improve. To do so, however, will draw in a range of other critical elements: the strengthening of civil society, the effectiveness of public services, the creation of adaptable institutions in the voluntary and community sector (including that special sector of 'social businesses'), and above all about the development within people of the softer skills of co-operation, collegiality and creativity. We need, in other words, to look to higher education to help us to grow social as well as human capital.

Universities and colleges are vital here too. Leaders on both sides need to manage Community–University Collaboration as well as Business–University Collaboration. David Watson's account of the challenges involved in this process is timely and helpful. It is based on his extensive experience at the University of Brighton – a pioneer in this field – as well as on sector-wide groups like the Universities UK (UUK) Longer-Term Strategy Group. Watson is particularly useful in reminding us about the necessity of strategic thinking (we need to develop 'intelligent' customers and suppliers in the community arena at least as much as for business and industry), about the centrality of values (and the academy's core business of knowledge creation and appraisal), and above all about the role of university staff, students and graduates in helping us to create not only a prosperous economy but also a cohesive community.

Richard Lambert
Director-General of the CBI
October 2006

# ACKNOWLEDGEMENTS

In researching and writing this book I have been aided and abetted by colleagues and friends all around the world. Key inspirations within the UK have been Rachel Bowden and Elizabeth Maddison of the University of Brighton, Professors Ron Barnett of the Institute of Education University of London, Dick Taylor of the University of Cambridge and Brian Ramsden. Brian was the founding chief executive of the Higher Education Statistics Agency (HESA), without whom the cause of reflective self-study in UK higher education would be significantly poorer. Internationally I have benefited from the wise counsel of Professors Ira Harkavy and Lee Benson of the University of Pennsylvania, Bruce Muirhead of the University of Queensland, Chris Duke of the Royal Melbourne Institute of Technology, and Maria Slowey of Dublin City University. Earlier versions of part of this material appeared in *Higher Education Review, Higher Education Management and Policy*, the *Higher Education Quarterly, Perspectives – Policy and Practice in Higher Education*, the Higher Education Academy (HEA) magazine *Academy Exchange, Ad Lib* (University of Cambridge), and the *Guardian Online*. I am grateful to those who listened to and commented on lectures and other presentations at the University of Cambridge Institute for Continuing Education, Oxford Brookes University, Wilton Park, New College Oxford, Tsinghua University (Beijing), the University of Warwick, the University of Wolverhampton, Birkbeck College, and the Institutional Management in Higher Education (IMHE) programme of the Organisation for Economic Co-operation and Development (OECD) in Paris, as well as the members of the Council of University Deans of Arts and Humanities (CUDAH – who had a particular influence upon the content and style of Chapter 9), and my students on the Master of

Business Administration (MBA) course in Higher Education Management at the Institute of Education (with special thanks to Emma Wisby for help with the issue of 'world-classness'). Thanks, too, to the University of Hertfordshire and Public and Corporate Economic Consultants Limited (PACEC) for permission to use Figure 9.13 and to Marilyn Wedgwood similarly for her two diagrams in Chapter 9.

I am grateful to the editors of this pioneering series – David Palfreyman and David Warner – for giving me a third chance to get it right. They will find that this volume returns to the tone and style of my first effort, on *Managing Strategy* (Watson 2000), rather than that of the more hands-on, tool-kit, which Elizabeth Maddison and I offered in *Managing Institutional Self-Study* (Watson and Maddison 2005). This is deliberate. I believe that commitments to civic and community engagement are a strategic matter, which go to the heart of the culture and values of any higher education institution (HEI). Consequently, getting this right is a matter of thinking clearly and understanding the strategic context, the opportunities and the constraints, in a sophisticated way, in addition to following the injunctions of self-study to surround operational decisions with evidence. If this is more of a ground-clearing than a 'how-to' volume, so be it (although institutions wishing to use it for benchmarking purposes are directed towards the self-evaluation questionnaire in Chapter 8). We can work on the practice together, across the sector, and through global networking.

The dedication to Lord Ron Dearing is not only in response to his personal encouragement and support over at least two decades, but also because of his staunch advocacy of the role of higher education in 'shaping a democratic, civilized, inclusive society' (NCIHE 1997: 72). The struggle continues.

Last but by no means least, Betty Pinto Skolnick continues to be my most important critical friend. None of those named is in any sense responsible for errors of fact, emphasis or judgement in anything which follows.

# ABBREVIATIONS

| | |
|---|---|
| A level | Advanced Level |
| ACU | Association of Commonwealth Universities |
| AHRC | Arts and Humanities Research Council |
| AAC&U | Association of American Colleges and Universities |
| ASN | additional student numbers |
| AUCEA | Australian Universities Community Engagement Alliance |
| AUQA | Australian Universities Quality Agency |
| BSCKE | Brighton and Sussex Community Knowledge Exchange |
| C&IT | communication and information technology |
| CaLD | cultural and linguistic diversity |
| CBI | Confederation of British Industry |
| CCP | Center for Community Partnerships |
| CENTRIM | Centre for Research into Innovation Management (University of Brighton) |
| CETL | Centre for Excellence in Teaching and Learning |
| CIHE | Council for Industry and Higher Education |
| CMU | Campaign for Mainstream Universities |
| CPD | continuous professional development |
| CUDAH | Council of University Deans of Arts and Humanities |
| CUDASSH | Council of University Deans of Arts, Social Sciences and Humanities |
| CUPP | Community–University Partnership Programme |
| DEST | Department of Education, Science and Training |
| DfES | Department for Education and Skills |
| DipHE | Diploma of Higher Education |
| EAP | English for Academic Purposes |

| | |
|---|---|
| ESF | European Social Fund |
| ESRC | Economic and Social Research Council |
| EU | European Union |
| EUA | European University Association |
| F4P | Football for Peace |
| F4U | Football for Unity |
| FE | further education |
| FEI | further education institution |
| Fd | foundation degree |
| GDP | gross domestic product |
| GCSE | General Certificate of Secondary Education |
| HCAT | Hastings College of Arts and Technology |
| HE | higher education |
| HE-BCI | Higher Education Business and Community Interaction |
| HEA | Higher Education Academy |
| HEACF | Higher Education Active Community Fund |
| HEI | higher education institution |
| HEFCE | Higher Education Funding Council for England |
| HEIF | Higher Education Innovation Fund |
| HEPI | Higher Education Policy Institute |
| HEROBAC | Higher Education Resources for Business and the Community |
| HESA | Higher Education Statistics Agency |
| HMO | houses in multiple occupation |
| IBL | industry-based learning |
| ICT | information and communication technologies |
| IBE | Institute of Business Ethics |
| IMHE | Institutional Management in Higher Education |
| IoD | Institute of Directors |
| KT | knowledge transfer |
| KTCF | Knowledge Transfer Capability Fund |
| MBA | Master of Business Administration |
| NEH | National Endowment for the Humanities |
| NGO | non-governmental organization |
| NHS | National Health Service |
| NSS | National Student Survey |
| NYU | New York University |
| OECD | Organisation for Economic Co-operation and Development |
| OFFA | Office for Fair Access |
| OU | Open University |
| PACEC | Public and Corporate Economic Consultants Limited |
| PQA | Post-qualifications admissions |

| P4P | Partnerships for Progression |
|---|---|
| RAE | Research Assessment Exercise |
| REMAS HE | Refugee Education Mentoring Advice and Support into Higher Education |
| RSA | Republic of South Africa |
| RT | Resilent Therapy |
| SCOP | Standing Committee of Principals (now Guild HE) |
| SEEDA | South East England Development Agency |
| SOAS | School of Oriental and African Studies |
| SOMUL | Social and Organisational Mediation of Learning |
| SPRU | Science Policy Research Unit (University of Sussex) |
| *THES* | *Times Higher Education Supplement* |
| TLRP | Teaching and Learning Research Programme |
| UCH | University Centre Hastings |
| UK | United Kingdom |
| UNI | Urban Nutrition Initiative |
| UQ | University of Queensland |
| USA | United States of America |
| UUK | Universities UK |
| WBL | wider benefits of learning |
| WEPIC | West Philadelphia Improvement Corps |
| WHOOP | Wellbeing, Health and Occupation for Older People |
| WP | widening participation |

# INTRODUCTION

*There is an international convergence of interest on issues about the purposes of universities and colleges and their role in a wider society. Much of this is structured around perceptions of the vital role of higher education in both sophisticated and developing knowledge economies. Meanwhile there has been a dearth of scholarly attention to the practice (as opposed to the rhetoric) of civic engagement by universities and colleges in various cultural contexts. This book attempts to fill the gap.*

The modern university is expected to be many contradictory things, simultaneously. Some of these are set out in Figure 1.1.

*Figure 1.1* Pressures on modern universities

- Conservative and radical;
- Critical and supportive;
- Competitive and collegial;
- Autonomous and accountable;
- Private and public;
- Excellent and equal;
- Entrepreneurial and caring;
- Certain and provisional;
- Traditional and innovative;
- Ceremonial and iconoclastic;
- Local and international.

As institutions, we are expected simultaneously to 'conserve' aspects of social tradition and to pose 'radical' alternatives. In doing so universities will be expected both to support and to provide a critical account of a whole range of activities from politics and policy-formation to social fashions. As for the relationships between higher education institutions, we are assumed both to supply a competitive market and to promote the interests of public education, including higher education in general. Meanwhile the institutions walking this tightrope will be both proudly autonomous and self-reliant, on the one hand, and bound into networks of accountability – including, critically, for the use of taxpayers' money – on the other. Indeed, when a university head is asked the difficult question 'is your institution in the public or the private sector?' the only sensible answer is 'yes'. This deep ambivalence extends into other broad aspects of expectation, inside and outside the system. Universities and their members are expected to strive for the best; to be in some essential respects elitist. At the same time, they and their backers are keenly aware of their responsibilities to society at large, to democratic progress, and to egalitarianism. In a related sphere, they will be enjoined to be aggressively entrepreneurial, to understand and exploit their assets; at the same time as holding a profound duty of care to their members, those who rely on them to deliver softer goods, and to society in general. In their core business – of knowledge creation, testing, and use – they will be looked to for authoritative, certain advice, while needing at the same time to promote the understanding that nearly all knowledge is provisional and subject to challenge and improvement; it is no accident that academics are notoriously more confident in expression the further they move away from their true fields of expertise. Institutionally, therefore, they will present a face to the world that is both traditional and innovative, as well as a mix of cultural contributions that is both highly ceremonial (as in the public rites of passage like matriculation and graduation) and prepared to be challenging and iconoclastic (in ways which successive generations of students in particular discover for themselves). Finally, nearly all higher education institutions will operate within a number of concentric spheres: their immediate locality; an economic region, whether formally defined or not; a home nation; and as members of the global family of universities and colleges.

What is interesting about this list is that it precludes any sense of the university being isolated from its community, of the 'ivory tower', or the 'castle in the swamp'. This book is about ways of understanding and relating to a wider set of relationships, summed up as civic and community engagement.

The working definition of 'civic and community engagement' used in this volume has several strands. It starts with the practical view of Bruce Muirhead (then of the University of Queensland, now Director

of Eidos – the Australian Consortium on Higher Education, Community Engagement and Social Responsibility), a leading Australian
advocate, who defines the concept as 'a collection of practices loosely
grouped under a policy framework designed to connect ... a university with its naturally constituent community' (Watson 2003: 16).
It connects with my own earlier work, in association with Muirhead
and others, leading to a description like the following. Civic engagement 'presents a challenge to universities to be of and not just in
the community; not simply to engage in "knowledge-transfer" but
to establish a dialogue across the boundary between the University
and its community which is open-ended, fluid and experimental'
(Watson 2003: 16).

Above all, members of the movement (if there is one such) are
conscious of its long provenance. As shown in the first chapter,
'community–university engagement' or 'civic engagement' is an increasingly salient objective for higher education institutions across
the world. It is also one which frequently resonates with a university's foundation and history. Deryck Schreuder, late of the
University of Western Australia, leads us back to Clark Kerr's 'multi-
versity', constructed in the USA in the years after the Second World
War: 'Newman's world had been stood on its head: Engagement was
the determining rationale for university operations, adaptation and
mission. The Idea of the University centred around the transfer of
knowledge, not its custodianship' (EUA/ACE 2004: 56).

By the turn of the twenty-first century, the relationship with society was considered to involve much more than 'transfer'. According to the Association of Commonwealth Universities (ACU),
'engagement is [now] a core value for the university'. In the Association's consultative paper, this proposition was unpacked as
follows:

> Engagement implies strenuous, thoughtful, argumentative in-
> teraction with the non-university world in at least four spheres:
> setting universities' aims, purposes and priorities; relating
> teaching and learning to the wider world; the back-and-forth
> dialogue between researchers and practitioners; and taking on
> wider responsibilities as neighbours and citizens.
>
> (ACU 2002: i)

At a conference on 'higher-education assisted community schools as
sites of civic engagement' in Philadelphia in March 2001, an international group of university leaders began to draft a 'Declaration of
Participatory Democracy' including the following aim:

As powerful, cosmopolitan, moral and intellectual enterprises dedicated to the betterment of humanity, universities are now uniquely capable of leading and sustaining a global social movement to accelerate human progress towards participatory democratic schooling systems and participatory democratic societies.

From this and other meetings in Philadelphia emerged the 'International Consortium for Higher Education, Civic Responsibility and Democracy' in association with the Committee on Higher Education and Research of the Council of Europe. In its mission the Consortium seeks to 'document, understand, and advance the contributions of higher education to democracy on the campus, in the local community, and the wider society'. The European and North American founder members have subsequently been joined by South Africa (through the Joint Education Trust), Australia and South Korea. The consortium itself has sponsored a pilot study on 'universities as sites of citizenship and civic responsibility'. For further information (and the source of these quotations) see http://iche.sas.upenn.edu/index/index.htm. In June 2006 a further version of the Declaration was affirmed by 150 university and government leaders in Strasbourg under the aegis of the Council of Europe Forum on Higher Education and Democratic Culture, and a website was launched at http://dc.ecml.at.

Meanwhile, in September 2005 Tufts University brought together leading figures from universities across the world at their conference centre in Talloires, in south-west France. The meeting resulted in another draft declaration 'on the civic roles and responsibilities of higher education'. It included the following practical injunctions.

- Expand civic engagement and social responsibility programs in an ethical manner, through teaching, research and public service.
- Embed public responsibility through personal example and the policies and practices of our higher education institutions.
- Create institutional frameworks for the encouragement, reward and recognition of good practice in social service by students, faculty, staff and their community partners.
- Ensure that standards of excellence, critical debate, scholarly research and peer judgement are applied as rigorously to community engagement as they are to other forms of university endeavor.
- Foster partnerships between universities and communities to enhance economic opportunity, empower individuals and

groups, increase mutual understanding and strengthen the relevance, reach and responsiveness of university education and research.

- Raise awareness within government, industry, charitable, not-for-profit and international organizations about higher education's contributions to social advancement and well-being. Specifically, establish partnerships with government to strengthen policies that support higher education's civic and socially responsible efforts. Collaborate with other sectors in order to magnify impacts and sustain social and economic gains for our communities.
- Establish partnerships with primary and secondary schools, and other institutions of further and higher education, so that education for active citizenship becomes an integral part of learning, at all levels of society and all stages of life.
- Document and disseminate examples of university work that benefits communities and the lives of their members.
- Support and encourage international, national and regional academic associations in their efforts to strengthen university civic engagement efforts and create scholarly recognition of service and action in teaching and research.
- Establish a steering committee and international networks of higher education institutions to inform and support all their efforts to carry out this Declaration.

The full Talloires Declaration can be accessed at www.tufts.edu/talloiresnetwork/TalloiresDeclaration2005.pdf.

At the time of writing the Talloires movement remains firmly on the road. Led by Susan Stroud (an important figure in several of the American initiatives discussed in Chapter 7, not least as founder and Director of Innovations in Civic Participation – see www.icip.org), the signatory institutions are being encouraged to 'conduct a self-assessment' of their civic engagement activities, to 'develop an institutional plan of action, and to share relevant parts of the plan with others in the Talloires network'. At the same time, planning proceeds on drawing all members into a single, concerted project on a global scale. The topic provisionally chosen is literacy (Gourley 2006; see also the report of the conference, Talloires 2005).

Most of the voices I have quoted so far have been from inside the academy. Their priorities are reinforced by two 'outside-in' perspectives. First there is the political and economic drive for utility. In 1997 the United Kingdom (UK) Dearing Committee quoted Robert Reich's *The Work of Nations* on this point:

The skills of a nation's workforce and the quality of its infrastructure are what makes it unique and uniquely attractive in the
world economy ... so important are these public amenities, in
particular the university and the airport, that their presence
would stimulate some collective analytical effort, even on a
parched desert or frozen tundra. A world class university and an
international airport combine the basic ingredients of global
symbolic analysis: brains and quick access to the rest of the world.

(NCIHE 1997: 190)

In responding to Dearing in their Green Paper, *The Learning Age*, the
UK government expressed a second, even wider, emancipatory hope
for lifelong learning, including the role of the universities. This softer
sense of engagement – based in the qualities higher education fosters
in individuals – is equally relevant to effective engagement.

As well as securing our economic future, learning has a wider
contribution. It helps make ours a civilised society, develops the
spiritual side of our lives and promotes active citizenship.
Learning enables people to play a full part in their community. It
strengthens the family, the neighbourhood and consequently the
nation. It helps us fulfil our potential and opens doors to a love of
music, art and literature. That is why we value learning for its
own sake, as well as for the equality of opportunity it brings.

(DfEE 1998: foreword)

So there is the challenge – from 'outside-in' and 'inside-out'. In this
book I attempt to assist not only the better understanding of these
forces, but also how we in the institutions can optimally respond to
them. Some suggestions are also made about how we should *manage*
the consequences.

The case studies at the centre of the book are limited by their
location in the English-speaking world of Anglo-American-
Australasian higher education. The special conditions of continental
Europe, of the accession states to the European Union, of Commonwealth countries from the Caribbean to Africa, of Latin America,
of the Indian sub-continent, and Asia, of the Pacific rim, and of the
contrasting global neighbours of Japan and the People's Republic of
China would each provide their own stories of how to fit university
development into twenty-first-century society, and are only alluded
to from time to time. However, in the concluding chapter, I have
attempted to draw some generic conclusions which I hope will
resonate with readers from these other important parts of an
increasingly interdependent world of global higher education.

# PART ONE: BACKGROUND

# 2

# CIVIC ENGAGEMENT AND THE FOUNDING OF MODERN UNIVERSITIES

*This chapter covers two main themes:*

- *the 'founding' intentions of universities and colleges in various eras and various countries, and how these have adapted to external pressures; and*
- *the role of higher education in contributing to human, social and creative capital, including a critique of each of these approaches.*

What have the Romans ever done for us?
                                        (*Monty Python's Life of Brian* 1983)

Institutions like universities carry considerable freight: today we are experiencing a flurry of interest in institutions as (in Samuel Scheffer's phrase) 'infrastructures of responsibility' (Williams 2006). As suggested in the Introduction (Chapter 1), modern societies have strong, sometimes contradictory, interests in both the purposes and the performance of their universities. More particularly, at the beginning of the twenty-first century there is evidence, all around the world, of renewed interest in the civic and social role of universities and colleges. Every week seems to bring a new conference, somewhere, on the theme and, in the spirit of David Lodge's wonderful character Morris Zapp, the temptation is to try to go to them all.

I say 'renewed' because a case can be made that the founding myths, and the constitutional origins of all but a very few universities are grounded in just such a role. Think of the poor scholars supported by the founders of Oxford and Cambridge Colleges, the local and regional ambitions of the Victorian civics, the confederations of professional schools that came together to form the British

Polytechnics and Central Institutions, and that is just in the UK. In the United States of America (USA), the origins of many now elite private institutions lay in creating cadres of clergymen, teachers, lawyers and doctors to serve colonial and then state communities; the 'land grant' universities were founded by direct investment of communities, mostly across the West, in creating useful knowledge; and so on.

One example will have to serve to demonstrate this rich legacy of community interest in university foundation. There follow some extracts from the Charter granted by Edward VII in 1905, to convert the University College of Sheffield (founded 1836) into the University of Sheffield. Several points are of note, including:

- the focus on teaching and vocational courses (in what is today a proud member of the 'research-intensive' Russell Group – note the order of the objectives in clause 14);
- the capacity to change the structure and focus, but not the core mission, of the institution;
- the desire to serve the special interests of local industry (like metallurgy);
- the implication of 'professional' oversight of 'technical attainments';
- the provision for examining, inspecting and generally engaging with other levels and types of education; and
- the modernity of seeking to ensure not only religious but also gender equality of both staff and students (a comparison with the twentieth-century history of the 'ancient' universities of Oxford and Cambridge is salutary).

Whereas Humble Petitions have been presented to Us by the University College of Sheffield and by the Lord Mayor Aldermen and Citizens of the City of Sheffield praying Us to constitute and found a University within the said City for the Advancement of Knowledge the Diffusion and Extension of Arts Sciences and Learning the Provision of Liberal and Professional and Technical Education and the furtherance of the objects for which the University College of Sheffield was incorporated by our Royal Predecessor Queen Victoria and to grant a Charter with such provisions therein in that behalf as shall seem to Us right and suitable.

Now therefore know ye that We by virtue of Our Royal Prerogative and of Our Special grace certain knowledge and mere motion by these Presents for Us Our Heirs and Successors will and ordain as follows:

1.  There shall be and there is hereby constituted and founded in Our said City of Sheffield a University by the name and style of 'The University of Sheffield' with Faculties of Arts Science Medicine and Applied Science and such other Faculties either in addition to or in substitution for the aforesaid Faculties or any of them as may from time to time be prescribed by Statutes of the University.

14. The University shall be both a teaching and an examining body and shall subject to the Charter and Statutes so far and to the full extent which its resources from time to time permit provide for:
a.  Instruction and teaching in every Faculty.
b.  Such instruction in all branches of education as may enable students to become proficient in and qualify for Degrees Diplomas Associateships and Certificates in Arts Pure Science Applied Science Commerce Medicine Surgery Law and all other branches of knowledge.
c.  Such instruction whether theoretical technical artistic or otherwise as may be of service to persons engaged in or about to engage in Education Commerce Engineering Metallurgy Mining or in other industries or artistic pursuits of the City of Sheffield and the adjacent counties and districts.
d.  Facilities for the prosecution of original research in arts Pure Science Applied Science Medicine Surgery Law and especially the applications of Science.
e.  Such fellowships scholarships exhibitions prizes and rewards and pecuniary and other aids as shall facilitate or encourage proficiency in the subjects taught in the University and also original research in all such subjects.
f.  Such extra University instruction and teaching as may be sanctioned by Ordinances.
g.  Examination and inspection of Schools and other Educational Institutions.

15. Degrees representing proficiency in technical subjects shall not be conferred without proper security for testing the scientific or general knowledge underlying technical attainments.

23. It is a fundamental condition of the constitution of the University that no religious test shall be imposed upon any person in order to entitle him or her to be admitted as a Member Professor Teacher or Student of the University or to

> hold office therein or to graduate thereat or to hold any
> advantage or privilege thereof.
>
> 24. There shall be no discrimination on the basis of gender in
>     respect of eligibility for any office in the University or for
>     membership of any of its constituent bodies or of admission
>     to any degree or course of study in the University.

For the full document see www.shef.ac.uk/calendar/incorp.html.

From time to time national systems have demonstrated what the
biologist Rupert Sheldrake calls 'morphic resonance': a species-wide
simultaneous discovery of a significant evolutionary turn. During
these phases, the same themes and similar structures have emerged
across the university world to support higher education in the
community. A powerful example is the 'university settlement'
movement at the turn of the twentieth century (Freeman 2004).
Others include the growth of university-sponsored science parks and
'incubators' in the 1980s and access-orientated 'summer schools' in
the 1990s.

## What is the university for? I Historical perspectives

University leaders can be extraordinarily ignorant (or perhaps just
tactically amnesiac) about what their institutions were originally put
there to do, and how they have progressively reinvented themselves.
  'The University,' says Frank Rhodes in *The Creation of the Future*, 'is
the most significant creation of the second millennium' (Rhodes, 2001:
xi). People inside universities generally agree. There is a basic cultural
assumption about what a university is, and a reasonably agreed
account of its outline history. That outline will generally include:

- the classical antecedents, reaching their height with the library of
  Alexander at Constantinople;
- the late medieval foundations, at Bologna and Paris, and a little
  later at Oxford and Cambridge;
- a period of gentle decline through the early modern period (while
  science developed very significantly outside the academy, and an
  entirely different form of scholarship flourished in the seminary –
  including the many American colleges which provided the foundation of the modern 'private' powerhouses of the United States'
  system);

- a very significant nineteenth-century surge of foundations, leading to relatively distinctive national systems (following Humboldt's Berlin in 1810, the University of London in 1836, and the Morrill Act in the USA in 1852 – the source of the 'land grant' universities, and a set of well-endowed American research institutions imitating the German model, beginning with Johns Hopkins in 1876);
- a late nineteenth-century and early twentieth-century vogue for community-based technical and vocational higher education, spreading round the world (including to Australia, Japan and China); and
- a patchwork of early and mid-twentieth-century developments, often involving changes of status (the latter accelerating in the final decades of the century).

This long narrative history is capable of sustaining several 'Whig' theories, encapsulating contending views of progress and development towards a preferred vision of the present. These include:

- the *liberal* theory of higher education as self-realization and social transformation, including latterly an element of social mobility and meritocracy (perhaps reaching its height, and certainly retaining its most important talisman in Cardinal John Henry Newman);
- the *professional formation* theory, identifying universities and colleges as providers of expertise and vocational identity, in some continuous (law, medicine and theology) and some new (engineering, science and public administration) areas; and
- higher education as a *research engine*, allied to regional and national ambitions for economic growth (in this area contemporary governments have rediscovered, rather than invented, priorities that were high over a century ago) – variations on this theme include higher education as a source of *business services*, and of *national pride*.

Each of these theories can, of course, be recast in a dysfunctional or negative light. The liberal aspiration can become a means of social selection and exclusion. Aggressively individualistic notions of advancement can lead to discrimation. Professionalism can lead to narrow and self-interested instrumentalism. Research can ignore some of its wider ethical responsibilities, and national pride can convert into short-term state priorities, and so on.

This book attempts to reformulate and endorse another consistent theme of value and identity for the higher education tradition and legacy: that of *civic and community engagement*. As Stephen Lay concludes in his elegant survey of this long history for the *Observatory for Fundamental University Values and Rights* (otherwise known as the *Magna Charta Universitatum*): 'the university should be valued as an intellectual resource of inherent social usefulness and admired as the model of a reasoned approach to life' (Lay 2004: 111). His recommendation is that the 'expectation of public service' should be added to the Charta (Lay 2004: 109). (For another elegantly brief account of global university history see Graham 2005: 7–26.) In Chapter 11, I attempt to weave this thread of engagement together with its 'liberal' counterpart.

## What is the university for? II Types of capital formation

At its heart the university is a reservoir of intellectual capital: its most fundamental purpose is about the creation, testing and application of knowledge. As a consequence the twenty-first-century pre-occupation with knowledge management ought to be highly congenial to the higher education enterprise. To probe this further, it is helpful to assess the types of intellectual capital apparently preferred (and potentially politically privileged) in the wider society.

Traditionally the battle lines have been drawn between an economically focused preoccupation with *human* capital, seeing qualified manpower as an essential element of growth, and a community-focused desire for enhanced *social* capital, seeing education at all levels as a way of solidifying cohesive norms of mutually satisfying behaviour.

A 'new kid on the block' is the theory of *creative* capital, associated in particular with the work of Richard Florida. Yet another recent invention is *identity* capital – comprising the attributes individuals need to 'intelligently strategise and make decisions affecting their life courses' (Côté 2002: 117).

Creative capital shares features of the two traditional models, but it emphasizes entrepreneurialism and innovation in particular on the economic side, and small-group, especially 'outsider' or mould-breaking, commitments on the social side. Essentially, Florida finds in the recent history of the USA both a new (Marxist-style) mode of production and a new (related) 'creative class'. These are people 'in science and engineering, architecture and design, education, arts music and entertainment, whose economic function is to create new ideas, new technology and/or creative content' (Florida 2002: 4, 8–9). According to his analysis they now comprise 30 per cent of all employed people (with a 'super-creative' core of 12 per cent), leaving only 20 per cent in the traditional working class, and a clear new majority in the fast-rising 'service class' of occupations like personal care, food service and new-style clerical functions such as call centres (Figure 2.1). There are several aspects of this story which are, I think, overdrawn, but the central thrust holds true. For a modern university vice-chancellor in the UK, it resonates with several facts: that the most entrepreneurial students are in the Faculty of Art and Design; that 1990s 'foresight' panels dominated by old men in suits entirely missed (and hence gave away) a potential international lead in animation and computer games; and that a ten-year long, highly prescriptive climb up the ladder to full status as a chartered electrical engineer is no longer as attractive to applicants as it once was. More recently Florida has sought to expand his analysis from the competitive advantage held by certain communities to the competitive battle for the creative edge between nations (Florida 2005).

*Figure 2.1*   The US class structure, 1900–99

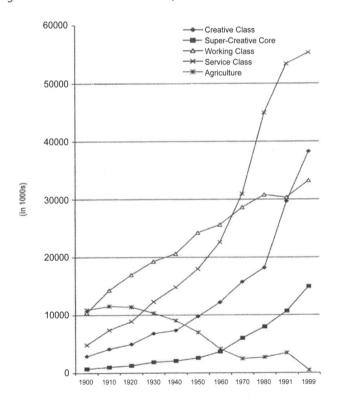

*Source:* Florida 2002: 75

A schematic comparison of the three contending approaches is set out in Table 2.1. Each can be analysed in terms of:

- the characteristic mode of analysis;
- the chief values implied;
- preferred indicators of performance;
- the key objectives; and, finally
- the form of mutuality or trust involved (for an excellent discussion of this dimension see Smith 2005).

*Table 2.1* Types of capital

| Human capital | Social capital | Creative capital |
|---|---|---|
| (Gary Becker) | (Robert Putnam) | (Richard Florida) |
| Individual agent | Networks and relationships | Clusters of creative people |
| Economic rationality | Shared values and norms | Diversity and tolerance |
| Educational duration/ qualifications | Mutual obligation Civic engagement | Low entry barriers for people |
| Individual income/ productivity | Quality of life | Rates of innovation |
| Self-interested trust | Normative trust | Affective trust |

*Source:* Based on Schuller 1998; Florida 2002; Smith 2005

In short, *human* capital analysis starts with the individual and his or her economic rationality, in the confident expectation that once simply aggregated it will produce a more productive and prosperous (usually national) society. Its advocates (like the economist Gary Becker) will count things like the duration of educational experience (especially initial, or 'compulsory' education) in order to assess relative performance. The trust it embodies is equally rational or calculated; it is the kind of trust you have in your bank, that it will not lose your money. *Social* capital (famously in the work of Robert Putnam) is an altogether softer concept, concerned fundamentally with quality of life. It focuses on social networks and relationships, and the kind of shared norms and values which they will represent. These emerge into patterns of civic and mutual obligation. Trust is equally normative: you cannot choose who constitute your significant others (and at the same time, the theory is sometimes criticized for its exclusionary possibilities – of minorities, and others who do not 'fit'). Finally, as introduced above, Florida's *creative* capital will cut across these larger social pictures and identify special 'clusters' of creative people; it is no accident that the theory has become associated with alternative and minority lifestyles, and can tend to stereotype groups like bohemians and gays. Diversity and tolerance are central, as are low barriers for entry (many of these clusters are rapidly established, and sometimes short-lived). The key indicator is rates of innovation; while the trust between members of groups is necessarily voluntaristic and hence affective, here you *can* choose your friends, partners and associates. Also, as hinted above, it works better on a sub-national (especially urban centre) basis, rather than for the whole region, or the nation state.

As the analysis in Chapters 9 and 10 confirms, these theoretical models matter. They represent a way of capturing priorities for the higher education enterprise which will have resonance for governments, for communities, and for the members of universities and colleges. Crudely (and in terms of their major emphases – of course, these interests overlap), governments want human capital, and communities want both this and the cohesive capital associated with social capital; modern students and their teachers (see the 'inner game' in Chapter 9) are increasingly interested in creativity and breaking the mould. Managing civic and community engagement will involve working across the range.

# 3

# THE UK: THE FATE OF THE DEARING COMPACT

*One of the strongest metaphors for the relationship between the state as a representative of the community and public services like the higher education system is that of a 'compact'. The idea is that of a clear set of reciprocal obligations between the universities, their communities and the state. This chapter tests the strength of this idea, through one of its most detailed, and apparently most fully politically endorsed elaborations: the post-Dearing settlement in the UK (NCIHE 1997).*

More broadly, the editors of a recent collection of essays on *Taking Public Universities Seriously* identify three big questions, with resonance all around the world. These are assessing public and private benefits in the context of 'who should pay?'; testing the priority, in a competitive and stretched world, of government investment in higher education; and weighing the 'appropriate balance between centralisation and decentralisation in the governance of the public university sector'. The notion at the heart of this discourse of a 'compact' between universities and the communities they serve on the one hand, and the state on the other, is apparently almost universally seductive (Iacobucci and Tuohy 2005: xi–xix).

## The search for a compact

The Dearing Committee was formed in the summer of 1996 in an atmosphere of crisis, and as a positive collusive political act between government and the official opposition, which successfully took the issue of higher education (and especially of fees) out of the

1997 election. The Dearing Report (NCIHE 1997) included 92 recommendations, brutally summarized in Figure 3.1.

*Figure 3.1*    Key messages in the Dearing Report

> - Greater use of communications and information technology;
> - A warning against cutting short-term funding;
> - Graduates from higher education to be expanded by 50 per cent – mainly at sub-degree level;
> - Tough measures to safeguard standards;
> - Enhanced professionalism in teaching;
> - New funding for research;
> - Students to contribute approximately £1000 per annum on an income contingent basis;
> - Stronger regional and community role for higher education;
> - A review of pay and working practices.

The Dearing Committee was accused by a number of commentators of 'lacking vision'. In most instances they simply meant that it lacked *their* vision. In our book, *Lifelong Learning and the University: A Post-Dearing Agenda*, published in 1998, Dick Taylor and I suggested that there were at least four sets of animating ideas. The first was the contribution of higher education to lifelong learning, as embedded particularly in the qualifications framework, views on articulation and collaboration between education sectors, and especially fairer and more effective support for all types of learners in higher education (HE). The second involved a vision for learning in the twenty-first century, as embodied in ideas about credit and the qualifications framework, assurance of standards as well as quality, teacher professionalism, communication and information technology (C&IT), key skills, and work experience. Funding research according to its intended outcomes came third, as set out in a multi-stranded model for research evaluation and funding; leading to rejection of the notion of a 'teaching-only' university. The final big idea was the compact itself, essentially a 'deal' whereby institutions retain their independence and gain increased security in return for clearer accountability (especially on standards) and greater responsiveness to a wide range of legitimate stakeholders (Watson and Taylor 1998: 151–2).

The Dearing Report delineated what it called a 'new compact' in some detail, as follows. Given that one of its central objectives was 'the creation of a civilised, democratic, inclusive society', I have identified (in italics) those parts of the deal which relate especially to civic and community engagement.

Society and taxpayers, as represented by the Government were seen to contribute:

- a fair proportion of public spending and national income to higher education; and
- greater stability in the public funding and framework for higher education.

In return they would receive the benefits of:

- *a highly skilled, adaptable workforce;*
- *research findings to underpin a knowledge-based economy;*
- *informed, flexible, effective citizens;* and
- a greater share of higher education costs met by individual beneficiaries.

Students and graduates would contribute:

- a greater financial contribution ... to the costs of tuition and living costs (especially for those from richer backgrounds); and
- time and effort applied to learning.

In return for:

- *more chances to participate in a larger system;*
- better information and guidance to inform choice;
- a high quality learning experience;
- a clear statement of learning outcomes;
- rigorously assured awards which have standing across the UK and overseas;
- fairer income contingent arrangements for making a financial contribution when in work;
- *better support for part-time study;* and
- larger access funds.

Institutions should supply:

- collective commitment to rigorous assurance of quality and standards;
- new approaches to learning and teaching;
- continual search for more cost-effective approaches to the delivery of higher education; and
- commitment to developing and supporting staff.

Their benefits should include:

- a new source of funding for teaching and the possibility of resumed expansion;

- new funding streams for research which recognise different purposes;
- *greater recognition from society of the value of higher education*; and
- greater stability in funding.

Staff in higher education contribute:

- commitment to excellence; and
- willingness to seek and adopt new ways of doing things.

They should receive in turn:

- *greater recognition (financial and non-financial) of the value of all of their work, not just research*;
- *proper recognition of their profession*; and
- fairer pay.

Employers should contribute:

- *more investment in training of employees*;
- increased contribution to the infrastructure of research;
- *more work experience opportunities for students*; and
- *greater support for employees serving on institutions' governing bodies.*

Their resulting benefits include:

- *more highly educated people in the workforce*;
- *clearer understanding of what higher education is offering*;
- *more opportunities for collaborative working with higher education*;
- *better accessibility to higher education for small and medium sized enterprises*; and
- outcomes of research.

Finally, families of students, while making a possible contribution to costs, should benefit from:

- *better higher education opportunities for their children*; and
- *better, more flexible higher education opportunities for mature students.*

(NCIHE 1997: 283; emphasis added)

The emphasized passages all underline the role of higher education in supporting civil society and the state, alongside the economy, and stress the values of fairness and accessibility, as well as the essential theme of public confidence. The fate of the compact has been, at best, mixed, not least in these regards.

## Whatever happened to the Dearing Report?

New Labour's first-term policy on higher education (New Labour Mark I) was structured around Dearing, with the exception of a serious modification of his recommendations on fees and student support, which has haunted them ever since. Essentially, the government was too greedy. Ministers took the Dearing recommendation of a student contribution to course costs and ignored what the report said about living costs, especially for poorer students. Simultaneously, they completed a Conservative project of turning all student grants into loans. This precipitate decision has become the Achilles heel of subsequent New Labour policy for higher education. Almost every major policy initiative, and certainly every discussion of how the system should be funded overall, has been drawn back into a kind of maelstrom of misunderstanding, of posturing and of bad faith about costs and charges to students, exacerbated by an aggrieved middle-class sense of entitlement.

The new government was, of course, almost immediately forced to trim: the student fee became means tested (in 2005–06 only about 40 per cent of students pay the full fee), but at the expense of immense bureaucracy and transaction costs; hardship funds were distributed via universities (but only after all loan facilities were taken up) – initially these were called 'access' funds because ministers had difficulty with the concept of 'hardship'; and 'specific' grants were progressively added to the mix (with the usual problem – the more precisely you set conditions for a benefit, the less likely it is to be taken up). Meanwhile, post-devolution Scotland decided to go a different way (rejecting upfront fees), and Wales would like to (but cannot apparently afford to).

Almost everything else in the Dearing Report, *Higher Education in the Learning Society* (NCIHE 1997), has come to pass, although not always exactly as intended (see Watson and Bowden 2000). This was a policy essentially 'with the grain' of a formally unstratified system and it reached its height in 2000 with David Blunkett's speech at Greenwich on 'Modernising higher education: facing the global challenge'. New Labour Mark I, as set out in Figure 3.2, recognized that the achievements of the sector as a whole depended on the nurturing of different types of institution with different missions, but fundamentally within sector-wide arrangements: for quality assurance, for funding, and for fair competition (including for research support). It resisted strong calls to 'put the polytechnics back in their box', and subsequent performance suggests that this was right. Indeed, one of the problems with the Blunkett speech was that it

*Figure 3.2*   David Blunkett's agenda for HEIs

- Balance teaching, research and knowledge transfer;
- Secure improved quality across each of these missions;
- Support wider participation and the drive for social inclusion;
- Expand into new markets;
- Preserve and enhance the sector's 'traditional scholarship role';
- Improve management capacity;
- Staff development;
- Accountability to government and society;
- Links with employers and others;
- Careers guidance and work placements;
- Utilize information and communication technologies (ICT) more systematically and effectively; and, not least,
- Tackle the unacceptable situation in terms of equal opportunities.

*Source:* Based on Blunkett 2000: 30

insisted on a universal agenda, that each institution should 'all do it all' (Watson 2002).

The change of emphasis was sudden, and caught many supporters by surprise. The country had, for example, been in serious 'read my lips mode' about the unacceptability of differential fees until well into the second term. The shunt arose from remarks by the Prime Minister, added at the last minute to his Labour Party conference speech in Brighton in September 2001, that there would be a review of student support. What emerged eventually was a much more comprehensive U-turn. One of the main intentions of the 2003 White Paper, *The future of higher education*, the 2004 Higher Education Act, and subsequent announcements (otherwise New Labour Mark II), appears to be the re-emergence of a re-stratified system, endorsed at the highest level. New Labour apparently wants to put the clock back.

Collectively the proposals set out in Figure 3.3 (p.24):

- replace a flat-rate system of student fees, with a 'variable' or 'top-up' regime;
- herald even greater concentration of public funding of research;
- begin to categorize institutions, as for example, 'research-intensive', or 'more focused on teaching and learning', or 'engaged in serving local and regional economies'; and
- dilute the controlled reputational range of UK universities by lowering the bar for university title and admitting new entrants to both university statuses, including a 'for profit' sector.

*Figure 3.3* 2003 White Paper main themes

- Six per cent increase in baseline funding, but heavily earmarked;
- Deregulation of fees (between £0 and £3000) from 2006, 'graduate contribution scheme', restoration of grants and grants for part-timers;
- 'Access agreements' and regulator (Office for Fair Access – OFFA);
- Concentration of 'R' funding, Knowledge Exchanges, Centres for Excellence in Teaching and Learning (CETLs);
- University status possible on undergraduate degree-awarding powers only;
- New Arts and Humanities Research Council (AHRC);
- Accreditation of teachers, the Academy for the Advancement of Learning and Teaching in Higher Education, and the Leadership Foundation;
- Expansion principally through Foundation Degrees;
- National survey of student views and published external examiners reports.

*Source:* DfES (2003)

The result, in January 2004, was one of the most compelling House of Commons battles of the Parliament (the anticipated showdown in the House of Lords, where much of the action on the preceding Conservative government's HE bills had taken place was, in contrast, a damp squib). The Prime Minister's reputation was on the line; concessions were made up to the last minute of the second reading debate in January 2004; the vote was extremely tight (a majority of five); and the result was a compromise which has been widely (and accurately) reported as really satisfying no one.

The new 'maximum' fee of £3000 has turned out in effect to be a revised flat-rate fee, with very few institutions charging less (notably Leeds Metropolitan and Greenwich, and none, so far, charging nothing). Indeed, by setting a low limit (evidence released under the Freedom of Information Act suggests that sums up to £5000 were mooted) and a very high parliamentary hurdle for its upwards revision (positive resolution by both Houses), it is hard to see that much has changed: except for the Exchequer, which will have to fund the institutions in advance of earning back the 'graduate contribution' (this is undoubtedly why ministers have so far failed fully to follow through on a commitment to extend the deferral elements of the scheme to part-time students). Certainly those expecting the 'cap' simply to disappear following a planned review in 2009–10 have underestimated the obstacles: not only the parliamentary hurdle and

Treasury nervousness, but also political will in general in this contentious area. In the meantime, this modest adjustment to what the Department euphemistically calls 'publicly planned funding' is accompanied by a huge paraphernalia of 'reviews', of transaction costs, and of regulation (notably OFFA, whose teeth – much talked up in the debate – have apparently been drawn).

The government wanted a 'market' and it now has one, but not where it was planned. Fees are not only almost uniform, but have the significant merit of being deferred (with income-contingent repayment after graduation). The serious competition will be over bursaries and other incentives, without much positive impact on widening participation. The most socially progressive institutions will feel obliged to recycle the greatest proportion of their additional fee income to needy students, while most of the relevant action will be about well-qualified students from well-informed families operating their own 'post-qualifications auctions'.

The brutal conclusion of an analysis of New Labour's record to date is about the failure of public funding (Watson and Bowden 2005), most notably in support of teaching. Table 3.1 demonstrates the long, sorry story of the 'unit of resource'. This is the element of the 'compact' which, perhaps predictably, has been most conspicuously lacking. Dearing did not stimulate a revival of investment, except in the highly significant area of infrastructural support for scientific research (and because of conditions about 'matching funding' there were also negative unintended consequences here). Public funding of higher education (including of student support) as a proportion of gross domestic product (GDP) remains in the bottom third of the OECD league, well behind our main competitors. It has also fallen significantly behind investment in other educational sectors (Table 3.2).

Some parts of the sector may be close to financial meltdown. It is becoming clear that a substantial minority of institutions are running accumulated deficits on the basis that additional fee income from 2006–07 will simply back-fill these rather than be available for the improvements students (as paying customers) will expect to see.

The temptation is to conclude that not much has changed; a 'traditional' system has simply got larger and less financially secure. There is also a sense that progress in key areas – including many of those which relate to equity – slowed during the last Parliament. Certainly, whether or not formally signed up to, the compact has failed to live up to its billing.

It is also relevant that the Parliament of 2001–05 was an even more than usually feverish one: with the response to international terrorism, the war in Iraq, foundation hospitals, and the ban on hunting

*Table 3.1* Unit of public funding of teaching, 1979–2005

| | | INDEX | |
|---|---|---|---|
| Year | University | HEFCE | Polytechnic |
| 1979–80 | 100 | | 100 |
| 1980–81 | 106 | | 99 |
| 1981–82 | 103 | | 94 |
| 1982–83 | 106 | | 89 |
| 1983–84 | 107 | | 82 |
| 1984–85 | 106 | | 79 |
| 1985–86 | 103 | | 78 |
| 1986–87 | 102 | | 79 |
| 1987–88 | 105 | | 76 |
| 1988–89 | 103 | | 75 |
| 1989–90 | 100 | 100 | — |
| 1990–91 | | 91 | |
| 1991–92 | | 86 | |
| 1992–93 | | 80 | |
| 1993–94 | | 75 | |
| 1994–95 | | 73 | |
| 1995–96 | | 70 | |
| 1996–97 | | 65 | |
| 1997–98 | | 64 | |
| 1998–99 | | 63 | |
| 1999–2000 | | 63 | |
| 2000–01 | | 62 | |
| 2001–02 | | 63 | |
| 2002–03 | | 59 | |
| (excl. private fees) | | | |
| 2003–04 | | 61 | |
| 2004–05 | | 61 | |
| 2005–06 | | 63 | |

*Sources:* CVCP 1995; UUK 2003

with dogs, to say nothing of the breakdown of the ideological 'marriage' at the heart of the government. New Labour's first Parliament had one Secretary of State for Education and Skills. Its second had three. Probably the most impressive was Charles Clarke, but even he betrayed the lack of a corporate memory about higher education policy by sending out his own quick-response 'consultation paper' (a technique for thinking time borrowed from one of his Conservative predecessors, Gillian Shephard). Within other countries the notion of all bets being off in terms of the direction of major public services, not just when governments change but when new ministers arrive

*Table 3.2*   Department for Education and Skills resource budget, 2001–06

|  | 2001–02 outturn (million) | 2005–06 plans (million) | % change 01/02–05/06 (cash terms) |
|---|---|---|---|
| Schools, including sixth forms | £3,491 | £6,899 | 98% |
| Higher education | £6,006 | £8,142 | 36% |
| Further education, adult learning and skills, and lifelong learning | £5,815 | £8,452 | 45% |
| Total DfES resource budget | £23,844 | £34,129 | 43% |

*Source:* Watson and Bowden 2005: 33

and have to 'read themselves' into the job, would seem extraordinary. Certainly, it indicates little confidence in an ongoing compact.

At the time of writing, there is a sense of both exhaustion and irritation in New Labour's third term in office. The key politicians would like higher education to revert to being 'finished business'.

It is no accident that the first 'letter of direction' from a new Secretary of State (subsequently reshuffled herself) to the Higher Education Funding Council for England (HEFCE) should be both late and short. Indeed, it is probably both the latest and the shortest of the genre established in 1988. On 31 January 2006 (these letters used to arrive in November) Ruth Kelly begins by acknowledging 'a new era with the introduction of variable fees and bursaries, and the abolition of up front charges to eligible students'. In this era she declares a wish 'to give the sector continued clarity about our strategic priorities'. These are expressed as follows:

> We do not expect all institutions to try to do the same thing to the same extent. The diversity within the Higher Education system is a strength, and we expect the Council to continue to use the various funding streams at its disposal to support excellence across the full range of activities which institutions undertake, whilst encouraging each institution to define and implement its distinctive mission.
>
> (Ruth Kelly to David Young, 31 January 2006)

She then proceeds to ask the Council to pursue 'two major priorities ... not just in the funding allocations it decides in the short term, but in developing strategy for the longer term'. The first is 'to lead radical changes in the provision of higher education in this country by incentivising and funding provision which is partly or wholly designed, funded or provided by employers'. The second is 'on widening participation in HE for people from low income backgrounds, where in spite of the recent progress we have made we do not perform well enough'. She concludes with reference to two other issues: 'reducing bureaucracy' and 'equality of opportunity' for HE staff. Collectively these themes provide a political context for several of the themes discussed in Chapters 9 and 10.

Meanwhile, there are clues about future directions for New Labour. We have a White Paper on further education (*Raising Skills, Improving Life Chances*) that has put Level 3 achievement back at the top of the agenda (DfES, 2006). The 2006 budget further consolidated the 'Science and Innovation Framework', by ring-fencing medical research funding across Whitehall and holding out the prospect of a post-Research Assessment Exercise (RAE), metrics-driven system of institutional funding for research. Finally, there is the commitment to a review in 2009–10 of the new funding and student support arrangements.

This relatively detailed history of a decade of national higher education policy demonstrates how expectations of a 'compact' between higher education and the state have foundered on a reef of political cynicism and academic unrealism. The outcome is a kind of cautionary tale for advocates of the HE civic agenda. New Labour inherited a massively expanded system of HE, and has (with the exception of selective investment in science) not really transformed it any serious way. They remain trapped in traditional dilemmas about funding and organization (where the politicians would like mission differentiation while institutions chase similar measures of esteem – as discussed below in Chapter 5). They have potentially created a monster in the model chosen for the 'graduate contribution', and certainly placed an unintended constraint on further equity through expansion (as well as their much-vaunted target of 50 per cent of each age cohort participating in HE). Above all, perhaps, in their obsession with the 'world-class' status of a very few institutions they have taken their eye off the ball of what the Dearing 'compact' really meant: the aim of a world-class sector of higher education, fit for the challenges of the twenty-first century (Watson 2006). The danger here is that civic engagement comes to be seen, uncompact-like, as a one-way street, with expectations of institutions unmatched by the structural public investment that would be necessary for it to be soundly delivered. It is part of the argument of this book that at at least one level this should not matter: higher education institutions should do the right thing (and the thing that in almost all cases they were founded to do) without the necessity of a politico-financial quid pro quo.

# 4

# UNIVERSITY CIVIC ENGAGEMENT IN A GLOBAL CONTEXT

*This chapter explores the implications for university civic engagement of the emergence of a 'global' sector of higher education, including the opportunities and threats it incorporates. It concludes by reviewing the role of civic and community engagement in establishing 'world-class' status.*

## A global sector

However, much they may trim and interfere at home, the governments of most advanced societies conceptualize international higher education as a simple and a relatively open market (not that this precludes domestic protectionism). In Great Britain, for example, the headline responses to the most recent OECD *Education at a Glance* survey were nearly all about the UK's 'slip' in the share of the market for international students from 16 per cent in 1998 to 12 per cent in 2002 (the headline in the *Financial Times* on 15 September 2004 was 'Competition slows lucrative foreign student share to 12%').

Such simplistic analyses not only undervalue the historical global role of higher education, which has been much more profoundly structured around cooperation and mutual support than competition and nationalistic breast-beating, but can also be allied with a naive, melioristic view of globalization. John Gray is among the contemporary social theorists reminding us that the march of global markets, and instant global communication, is neither uniform nor universal. In his words, 'globalisation occurs largely in the realm of virtual reality and leaves much of everyday life untouched', while in its current phase globalization 'universalises the demand for a better life without supplying the means to satisfy it'. Further, 'because the global production system transcends national boundaries, no one is responsible for ensuring that it is safe' (Gray 2006: 20, 23). Higher education has a role in assisting our understanding of these dilemmas, and finding ways of overcoming them. Certainly, it should be no part of the mission of an individual university – still less of a national system – simply to drive the competition out.

Meanwhile, as the data in Table 4.1 shows, the exposure of UK higher education to its international business is considerable, and not solely about student fees. These effects, of course, are not felt evenly. Looking at international contributions to total institutional income, there is a significant minority of institutions under 5 per cent and another above 15 per cent in Figure 4.1. Figure 4.2 demonstrates that the institutional slope is steeper if just student fees are considered.

*Table 4.1* International sources of income, 2003–04 (£k)

| | | |
|---|---:|---:|
| *Research grants and contracts* | | |
| European Commission | 177,775 | |
| Other EU government | 6,138 | |
| EU other | 34,259 | |
| Other overseas | 130,013 | |
| Sub-total research grants and contracts | | 348,185 |
| | | |
| *Other services rendered* | | |
| EU government | 53,743 | |
| EU other | 8,107 | |
| Other overseas | 32,481 | |
| Sub-total other services rendered | | 94,331 |
| *Overseas (non-EU) student fees* | | 1,085,437 |
| *Total overseas income* | | 1,527,953 |

*Source:* UUK 2005: 47

We also have to consider market sensitivity and risk. As Figure 4.3 shows, students from East Asia and the Pacific (including predominantly China) just outnumber those from the European Union (EU). A 'wobble' in recruitment from the People's Republic of China in 2006 entries caused the Higher Education Policy Institute (HEPI) to consider just how exposed individual universities might be, with alarming results (HEPI 2006).

*Figure 4.1* Institutional spread of percentage income received from overseas sources, 2003–04

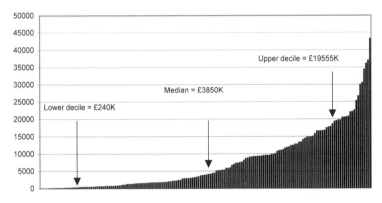

*Source:* UUK 2005: 47

*Figure 4.2* Income from overseas (non-EU) student fees, 2003–04

*Source:* UUK 2005: 63

Meanwhile, an exclusive focus on the 'bottom line' demonstrates the danger of ignoring other important perspectives:

- the ethical dimensions of a global university system;
- other political issues which may intrude (such as security);
- the cultural position of higher education in different national and regional contexts; and
- the effect upon their own institutions of recruitment of 'international' students.

*Figure 4.3* Sources of students in the UK by world region, 2003–04

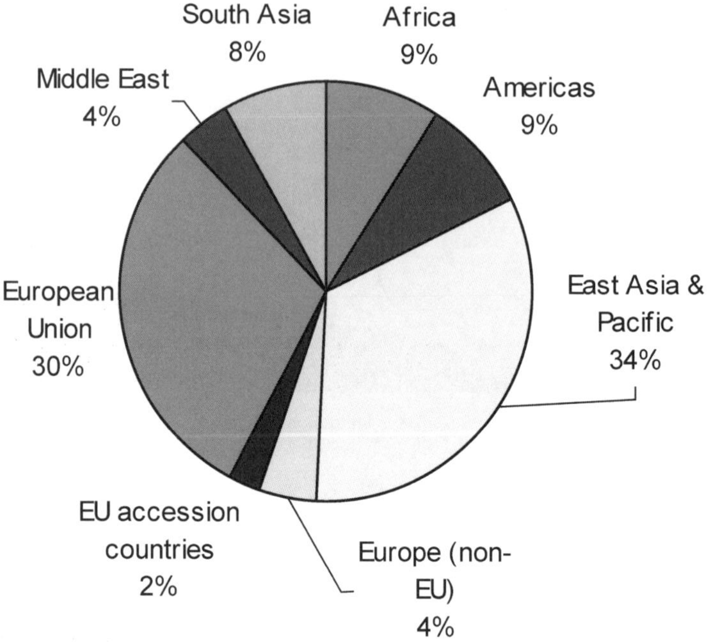

South Asia
8%

Africa
9%

Middle East
4%

Americas
9%

European
Union
30%

East Asia &
Pacific
34%

EU accession
countries
2%

Europe (non-
EU)
4%

*Source:* UUK 2005: 26

These are all angles from which we should begin to query the obsession with the bottom line, and at least some are alluded to in the Department for Education and Skills (DfES) strategy, *Putting the World into World-class Education* (DfES 2004c).

From the ethical point of view there are questions about the mutual support between national systems of higher education at different stages of development; of the asset-stripping of key personnel; of a potentially pre-emptive 'western' model of intellectual property registration; and of 'dumping' of poor quality e-learning materials. Interestingly, the development economists, as well as university leaders, are shifting focus from an analysis of 'brain drain' to 'brain gain'. At the ACU conference in Adelaide in 2006, Nadeli Pandor, Education Minister of the Republic of South Africa, urged delegates to consider the contribution made by emigrant professionals to their countries of origin: 'to have a meaningful developmental impact, this contribution would need to be nurtured and sustained to the point that we will begin to speak about brain circulation and not about brain drain' (see O'Leary 2006: 11). In other words, intellectual remittances are potentially as important as the funds sent home by emigrant workers.

From a political perspective, ethnic preferences, security sensitivities, or simply statist *force majeure* can undermine key academic values, while the role of higher education in both supporting and criticizing aspects of civil society can lead to confusion (Slowey and Watson 2003: 162–3, see also May 2004).

There is a particular resonance to my third question (about cultural contexts) as New Labour has put the concept of 'under-represented groups' on the face of its 2004 Higher Education Act (the issue of widening participation – WP – is discussed in more detail in Chapter 10).

## The international campus

Above all, we have yet to work through the full implications of an increasingly cosmopolitan staff and student community within the modern university. As Table 4.2 demonstrates, UK university campuses are now inescapably international.

*Table 4.2*   The international campus: institutions by number of overseas countries supplying students, UK, 2004–05

| | |
|---|---|
| >150 | 3 |
| 100–149 | 75 |
| 50–99 | 45 |
| 20–49 | 32 |
| <20 | 13 |

This rapidly changing internal demography raises some important issues:

- about pedagogy – as institutions need to deal with varied patterns of preparation for UK-based academic discourse (through programmes in study skills, English for Academic Purposes – EAP – and the like);
- about the curriculum – as subjects can clearly draw upon a wider range of international exemplifications of process, and area-specific controversies;
- about genuine cultural diversity – as some parts of university life can, without care, become enclaves of immigrants from specific societies;

- about conflict – as domestic and regional controversies from elsewhere in the world can be imported onto the campus (notably at present from the Middle East – see Polly Curtis of the *Guardian* on the recent controversies at the School of Oriental and African Studies – SOAS – Curtis 2005);
- about economics – through the need to manage risk across a variety of markets without becoming over-dependent on any single source (China – still essentially a command economy – could turn off the tap just as easily as it turned it on); and
- about values – the big question remains how representative of its host society a university should strive to be in this global context, especially since almost all higher education communities are likely to be more ethnically and religiously mixed than both the nation and the neighbourhood in which they find themselves.

Ideally, of course, the ethical argument and the economic drivers would coincide. Here there are some promising conclusions from a study commissioned by the Council for Industry and Higher Education (CIHE). A survey of the views of 'a wide range of multinational businesses on the competitiveness of UK higher education' concluded that one of the most significant competitive advantages lay in its pedagogical approach, with graduates relatively 'strong at creativity, at challenging received wisdom and assumptions or developing solutions based on a fusion of multi-disciplinary and multi-cultural views' (Brown and Ternmouth 2006: iii, 2).

The fundamental challenge is a very simple one, put most eloquently by Martha Nussbaum. It is about developing alternative narrative abilities on the part of both teachers and students: in particular 'the ability to think what it might be like to be in the shoes of a person different from oneself' (Nussbaum 2002: 289). This lies at the heart of managing engagement with the global community.

## What do we mean by world class?

And then there is a big distraction. There is no doubt that around the world national prestige is seen as bound up in success in an international competition to have some universities recognized as 'world class'. Meanwhile, it is clear that the results of the competition domestically have huge political and affective power, weak though both the conceptual and empirical basis of the exercise may be.

Is world class a *standard* (in which case we can all theoretically meet it)? Or is it a limited set of medals at the end of a *race* (or positions at the top of a league table)? If it is the latter, how long can we be champions before we have to put our title at risk again?

There are broadly two approaches to the definitional question. The *objective scoreboard* approach attempts to find and apply as neutral and consistent a set of statistics about performance as possible. This reaches its height in the Shanghai Jiao Tong list of the world's 'top 500' (first published in 2003). The *subjective beauty contest* approach may acknowledge some vital statistics in terms of the entry into the competition but will rely heavily on insider opinion. The London *Times Higher Education Supplement*'s (*THES*'s) 'World Rankings' has rapidly become the brand leader here. (Interestingly, in the summer of 2006, *Newsweek* has tried to combine the two: see the item 'Global Universities', in the joint issue for 21 and 28 August).

(A third approach, with significantly less influence, is to focus on institutions' relative presence on the Internet. 'Webometrics' uses the top Internet search engines to count online publications and cross-citation – see www.webometrics.info/. It thus ranks essentially in terms of web publication and Open Access initiatives. 'G-Factor' analyses the links between university websites only to create an internal popularity index of the sites themselves – see www.universitymetrics.com/g-factor.)

The Shanghai methodology is to assemble the weighted data in Table 4.3. Of the top 20 in their initial list, only four were in Europe and all of them in the UK. Cambridge was third after Harvard and Stanford, and Oxford eighth, after another four American institutions. The first Japanese university was Tokyo at 14. The first continental European institution was the Swiss Federal Institute of Technology in Zurich at 28. The Australian National University was at 53, Moscow State at 66, and the Hebrew National University at 90. There was no Chinese university in the initial top 100.

In contrast, the *THES* relies for at least half of its algorithm upon subjective opinion. In 2004 50 per cent of the score was based on academic peer review (1300 respondents from 88 countries). In 2005 this element was reduced to 40 per cent, but the balance (10 per cent) was made up by another beauty contest: 333 major employers were invited to 'identity up to 20 universities whose graduates they prefer to employ most'. The remaining half of the calculation is shown in Table 4.4. The *THES* uses citation data from the Essential Science Indicators database produced by Thomson Scientific (formerly the Institute of Scientific Information, www.isinet.com). A ten-year period is used for the analysis, with a lower cut-off of 5000 papers to eliminate small specialist institutions. An interesting further element is the 20 per cent of the total score based on the faculty-to-student ratio. While variations in institutional practices and international

*Table 4.3*   Shanghai Jiao Tong, 'world class' indicators, 2004 and 2005

| Criteria | Indicator | Code | Weight |
|---|---|---|---|
| Quality of education | Alumni of an institution winning Nobel Prizes and Fields Medals | Alumni | 10% |
| Quality of faculty | Staff of an institution winning Nobel Prizes and Fields Medals | Award | 20% |
| | Highly cited researchers in 21 broad subject categories | HiCi | 20% |
| Research output | Articles published in *Nature and Science (N&S)** | N&S | 20% |
| | Articles in Science Citation Index-expanded, Social Science Citation Index, and (2005) Arts and Humanities Citation Index | SCI | 20% |
| Size of institution | Academic performance with respect to the size of an institution | Size | 10% |
| Total | | | 100% |

*Note:* * For institutions specializing in humanities and social sciences such as London School of Economics, *N&S* is not considered, and the weight of *N&S* is relocated to other indicators.

*Source:* For details, see http://ed.sjtu.ed.cn/ranking.htm.

employment law make staff numbers less than completely comparable across the world, the *THES* maintains that this indicator is a simple and robust one that captures a university's commitment to teaching. (The *Newsweek* 'marriage', referred to above, further cements US domination: Cambridge and Oxford drop to sixth and eighth respectively, behind Harvard, Stanford, Yale, the tiny California Institute of Technology, and Berkeley.)

More generally, world class is one of those things which apparently you know when you see it. It is also more often asserted than proved. For an example, the members of the *Universitas 21* network of self-identified 'leading research intensive universities' come in at the following points on the initial Shanghai list: 36, 47, 80, 82, 92, 93, 110, 127, 145, 150, 187, 223, 241, 258, 314, and nowhere (see www.universitas21.com/memberlist.html).

*Table 4.4   THES* – summary table showing weightings for 2004 and 2005

| Criteria | Year | |
| --- | --- | --- |
| | *2004* | *2005* |
| Peer review | 50 | 40 |
| Citations per staff member | 20 | 20 |
| Staff-to-student ratio | 20 | 20 |
| Percentage of international staff | 5 | 5 |
| Percentage of international students | 5 | 5 |
| Employer ratings | — | 10 |
| Total | 100 | 100 |

*Source:* www.thes.co.uk/worldrankings/

There is a symmetry here with the ways in which national league tables are constructed around the world. *Whole institution* rankings tend to be constructed by newspapers on the basis of multiple indicators joined together by an algorithm which will privilege some forms of performance over others. Normally this will involve scoring ordinal rankings, as a result of which minute differences in real performance can often be transformed into rigid hierarchies of status. Meanwhile *subject or disciplinary* rankings are normally based on peer opinion, often around vague propositions about 'leadership' and with loose rules about timescales. For both of these reasons (the locality of the data in the first case, and the parochialism of the latter), league tables have, until recently, tended to be national sports (like the American World Series in baseball). An exception, which could be said to prove the rule, is the competition between a very small number of elite business schools, all chasing the international 'sponsored-executive' market (for example, see the Social Science Research Network's 'Top Business School rankings' at http:// ssrn.com). In this race indicators like the premiums on graduate salaries are especially important.

The types of outcome also vary. For example, it is striking how consistent national whole-institution rankings are over time, and how extremely volatile the international variants have proved to be in a very short time. The geological strata of the UK's *Times League Table* has hardly changed over a decade (and can be comfortably predicted simply by dividing student enrolments by total income – Rachel Bowden and I have devised the 'Prosperity Index' to capture this effect, see Watson and Bowden 2002: 31). Meanwhile shifts between rounds one and two of both the Shanghai and *THES* world rankings have sent some institutions into paroxysms of joy and others into the slough of despond. Classic examples of the former are Duke University, which rose to eleventh in the *THES* rankings for 2005 from outside the top 50, and Bristol, up more than 40 places to enter the top 50. Meanwhile ETH Zurich lost its top ten spot in the *THES*, and Sussex University, which had devised a promotional strategy around being '58th in the world' dropped to 100.

Distinctions between these different rules, scope and eligibility are important. Institutions need to know if they are entering one competition, or several. It is tactically important to know whether there is a single set of rules, or several; and, if the latter, how far we can afford to fall behind in any of them while 'winning' in others.

We may also need – inside the higher education sector – to sit back, think about what is going on, and curb our enthusiasm for the competition, especially if it can be proved that what we are engaged in is neither rational and scholarly, nor useful for any of our core purposes.

To return to the state of the art as regards establishing world-class status. I have attempted some quick and dirty content analysis of such claims. The following attributes of the 'world-class university' appear to be ubiquitous, probably in declining order of importance:

- what it does in research (especially Nobel prizes and the like);
- how it is regarded by its host society, including in the popular media;
- where its graduates are (especially in government and as captains of industry – leadership in other branches of the 'public service' is much less highly regarded);
- an attractive physical presence, including some prestigious buildings and other infrastructure (for example, libraries and other collections);
- international recruitment at postgraduate level (high-volume undergraduate recruitment from overseas, can in contrast, be seen as a 'non-selective' weakness).

And, curiously, not much more. Many of the 'common-sense' elements of high performance by comprehensive universities – like teaching quality, widening participation and social mobility, services to business and the community, support of rural in addition to metropolitan communities, as well as contributions to other public services – are conspicuously absent. In a similar, but much more scientific survey, the Canadian scholar Daniel Lang has reached exactly the same conclusion about the centrality (if not the exclusivity) of the research category. As he writes: ' "world-class" comparisons of research quality and productivity are possible, but ... any broader application to the "world-class" quality will be at best futile and at worst misleading' (Lang 2005: 27, 50).

However, perhaps the most important moral of this story is that you cannot be world class without history. The 'new entrant' (or even the relatively young institution) is virtually an impossibility at the highest level. A rare example of a university attempting – with some success – to buy its way into the premier league is provided by New York University (NYU). David Kirp has recently analysed how it recovered from the edge of bankruptcy in 1975 through a combination of aggressive fund-raising and highly selective investment. In this process it broke all the rules of elite American universities about not spending more than a small proportion of what it raises. As Kirp (2005: 14) states, 'NYU, impatient for success, opted for the "spend it now" approach'. The selectivity was tactical:

> In determining its priorities, NYU opted not to break the bank with investments in big science, focusing instead on some of the professional schools and liberal arts departments. The most dramatic transformation came in philosophy ... In 1995, the university lacked an accredited Ph.D. program in philosophy; five years later, it was ranked number one.
>
> (Kirp 2005: 14)

But this is an example which proves the rule. An additional hard fact is that governments have very little immediate influence over the informal rating. This is a long-haul proposition. The same may well be true of systems (as discussed below).

In business terms, the guru of 'world class' analysis is Rosabeth Moss Kanter, author of *World Class: Thriving Locally in a Global Economy*. Kanter's clue, including for universities, has to be in the subtitle: to quote one of her central questions 'what is the meaning of community in a global economy?' Juxtaposing 'cosmopolitans' and 'locals' in the fields of 'thinking', 'making' and 'trading', Kanter's secret formula is about ensuring that local activities meet world standards of excellence (Kanter 1995: 13, 21, 28, 30). For example, Leeds Metropolitan University is striving to be a 'world-class regional university'. How do you become world class at what it is you do, where you are, and with what you are given, rather than by slavish (and invariably doomed) imitative behaviour?

This is where the formal and informal world-class criteria set out above may be most damaging. Universities have vital roles in the twenty-first-century knowledge economy, and in society, that go beyond chasing the relevant suite of scores. Such roles include supplying qualified professionals, and supporting professions with research and development, in all sorts of areas that may not be sufficiently glamorous to attract the world-class ratings, especially in the public service. They may involve cooperating, rather than competing, with other higher education institutions to meet specific local and regional needs. They will sometimes imply putting a wider public interest above a particular institutional advantage, as discussed below.

In the mean time, whose interests does world-class status apparently serve? Who cares about whether or not it is achieved? It is a certainly an area characterized by deep ambivalence. As Anthony Stella and David Woodhouse of the Australian Universities Quality Agency (AUQA) conclude, in wide-ranging survey:

> People are already saying 'rankings are here to stay', and often in the same breath as they complain about the rankings. Merely to accept them as a given is analogous to observing that 'nuclear weapons are here to stay' but then use this as a reason not to work for their containment and limitation.
>
> (Stella and Woodhouse 2006: 22)

Governments (as suggested above) care deeply.

Institutions who consider themselves world class care, although perhaps not quite as much as their governments: to extend the (inevitable) sporting metaphor, the genuinely top performers do not appear to strain. Perhaps those who expend most energy in the quest are the 'aspirants' just outside this magic circle; certainly they are most prone to assert their claims by denigrating the competition.

Consumers (especially indebted ones) care. It has become a truism that they will, in most circumstances, select 'reputation' rather than objectively-measured 'quality' or 'performance' when deciding where to study.

League table compilers care; they sell an awful lot of magazines and newspapers.

However, is the resulting race good for higher education: for its internal development or for its external reputation? At its most generous it is an inexact science. To achieve scientific respectability it might have to concede a number of reforms which would reduce the enthusiasm of the main protagonists. Examples are devising 'value-added' scores, in order to establish what institutions have managed to do with differing input values (such as the prior attainment and background of students). Incidentally, this is a familiar trajectory for established league tables, as anyone familiar with English schools and universities will confirm. A genuine international competition would also presumably take account of different levels of state subsidy (as in European Commission competition rules). To quote Daniel Lang (2005: 42) again: 'unless one presumes that every university has the same mission, and every university has the same access to resources, inter-institutional comparisons – can fail'. Could there ever be a 'level playing-field'?

Where is the *public interest* in any of this (see also the discussion in Chapter 10)? Here the trickiest issue is undoubtedly the differing claims upon the university system made by the state and by civil society. Broadly there is a western assumption that universities are, in the words of Michael Daxner, former rector of the University of Oldenburg (and EU Education Commissioner in Kosovo) about 'society-making' rather than 'state-making'. In his words, 'we are needed because of our dangerous knowledge' (EUA/ACE 2004: 68). By 'dangerous knowledge', Daxner means the kind of principled critique which is enabled by academic freedom.

Such knowledge may be most sensitive, in particular times and places, for the state itself; not least because of its frequent role as a majority investor. There is perhaps an irony in the fact that around the world, as state investment reduces as a proportion of income earned by universities, so does government interest in steering the system increase.

Cultural contexts are vital. Higher education systems are just as 'culturally embedded' as other markets. In the words of John Kay's *The Truth about Markets*: 'This book is about the institutions that define our economic lives. It will become apparent that it is not just economic institutions which matter. Economic institutions function only as part of a social, political and cultural context. This is what I describe as the embedded market' (Kay 2003: 19). What works in Switzerland will not work in Botswana. Patterns of obligation and expectation are fused together.

In relation to the 'world class' ambition, the case of China is a particularly interesting worked example. The government has announced the intention of building some universities into world-class institutions, and related budgetary plan, including those associated with Projects 211 (1995 – 'one hundred first class universities for the twenty-first century') and 985 (1999 – for developing 'world-class universities and world-famous research universities') (Zhou Ji 2006: 36, 40). Beijing University, on the occasion of its 100th anniversary in 1998, and Tsinghua, on its 90th in 2001, were among those identified (Duan 2003). Germany is the first western country to follow suit, with the three winners of its 'excellence' initiative (Kahlsruhe, the Technical University of Munich, and the Ludwig-

Maximilians-University of Munich) announced in October 2006 (Labi 2006).

But the cultural specificity counts. Robert Skidelsky – a key interpreter of China to the UK – has reminded us that the term 'laissez-faire' (a western cliché for the free market) is translated into Chinese as 'wu wei' or 'active inactivity'. The metaphor is from gardening and implies growth managed by gentle but strategic pruning (Skidelsky 2006). Sun-Yu Pan's study of Tsinghua shows the gardeners in action, allowing growth in areas such as diversity of recruitment, international alliances, use of the English medium of instruction, and so on, while both the state and the university know that there will be limits to strategic freedom and autonomy (Pan 2006; see also Jessop 2006). Daniel Bell has recently explored these nuances from the perspective of a western teacher (Bell 2006).

There are some genuine dilemmas here, especially for the state and for the leaders of universities. For the state, as I have tried to establish:

- you cannot (apparently) 'buy' world-class status (although you can act to make it impossible, for example by inhibiting the creativity of the university);
- you cannot influence the judges (at least not very much – and even less beyond your national boundaries);
- you cannot just declare world-class status (at least without running the risk of looking silly); and above all
- you cannot simply 'manage' this status from outside – indeed the more you appear to do so, the less successful you are likely to be; the hard thing is that, because of the peculiar nature of the academic community, for it to be really successful you have to *trust* it to do the right thing (that is, to pursue its core mission of knowledge creation, testing and use, without fear or favour).

This is not to say that investment is unimportant. As Professor Alison Wolf has recently written in the *Times Higher Education Supplement*, 'Governments do construct successful universities'. The examples she gives are the California State system, the University of Texas at Austin and the nineteenth-century foundation of Göttingen in Hanover. However, she continues 'Universities thrive only if they are also given large amounts of academic freedom and operate in an academically competitive environment'. 'But,' she concludes, 'money never hurts' (Wolf 2006: 13).

To return to the case of China. Developed economies and societies generally look for two things from their higher education systems: first, a sound and 'comprehensive' contribution to economic development and social cohesion; and, secondly, a high level of achievement and esteem in what are seen to be international competitions for prestige. The former seems to require a high level of *planning*, in the interests of equity as well as efficiency. The latter is much less susceptible to 'planning'. It will require innovation and experimentation; its exact nature will be unpredictable, even serendipitous. There is an international consensus that the 'winners' here are frequently so because they have been entrusted with very significant *autonomy*.

Both domains, of course, require investment. However, in the former (social and economic contribution), outputs (returns on investment) can be more readily assured and accountability established. In the latter (peer recognition of high quality), there will have to be greater tolerance of devolved decision-making, and an acceptance that outcomes cannot be guaranteed. Some returns on investment will necessarily be minimal and others spectacular.

China wishes to be active and successful in both domains, but it has chosen a single approach for them both: that of central planning, and of investment and strategic decisions being made *for* rather than *by* the individual institutions, including those identified as flagships for the second domain. What is more, the investment may be abortive. Daniel Lang quotes Philip Altbach's conclusion that 'being world-class might not be affordable' (Altbach 2004: 5).

Another complication is the choice of terms like 'excellence' and 'world class' as if they are associated only with the second domain. A higher education system can be both excellent and world class in delivering the first (social and economic returns). It may only be so (this is another, potentially unpopular, 'international' hypothesis) if contributions are made to the first (societal) domain by *all* institutions on the basis of mutual respect and shared responsibility.

Meanwhile, for the individual university, the key points appear to be about:

- balancing ambition and realism;
- understanding your own business (which, critically, involves history); and
- tackling the most difficult question thrown up by mature institutional self-study – not 'how good are we?' but 'how good could we be?'

This is where mission differentiation, together with issues of complementarity, comes in. All over the world, governments would like to secure rational mission distribution (and hence, they think, ease

funding pressures); all over the world institutions of higher education (above a certain level of scope and activity) seek similar measures of esteem. This is why governments endlessly tinker with
frameworks: those with 'binary systems' think they should be dis-
solved; those without them think they should be created. Sometimes
(as has happened in Australia) a new system is tried and then
changed back.

The former (governments) have tried almost everything: exhorta-
tion, bribery, and punishment for non-compliance. An interesting
recent example of the first two of these in combination is the Higher
Education Funding Council for England's appeal for volunteers
among 'HEIs on the journey towards making the third stream their
second mission focus (after teaching)' (Circular Letter 05/2006, 30
March 2006).

The latter (the institutions) will do almost everything in order not
to cut themselves off from entry into the competitions where genuine reputational advantage is seen to lie, especially in research. Thus
several attempts to reform what is generally regarded as the bur-
eaucratic monster of the British Research Assessment Exercise have
foundered on the non-cooperation of university leaders who, like
managers of Premier League football clubs, have to believe that they
will win, sooner or later and whatever the odds. Thus the suggestion
in the Dearing Report (NCIHE 1997) that institutions should be
given incentives (and some kind of 'moral hazard') to stay out of the
RAE, the proposal in the Roberts Review (HEFCE 2003) that provision
should be segregated down different channels in order to
concentrate the efforts of the exercise where they are most needed,
and the latest initiative by the Chancellor of the Exchequer, in his
budget speech for 2006 that the 2008 exercise could be replaced by a
much simpler, 'metrics-based' desk exercise, have all been shouted
down.

The immediate practical answer for university leaders seems to be
to identify their own institution's zone of freedom of action, and to
decide how to use it. The temptation is (to borrow a sporting metaphor), to fail to play your own game.

In more constructive terms, I believe that these dilemmas inspire a
kind of reflective pragmatism (Watson 2000: 87). It means, for example, being serious about who your university's stakeholders really
are (those who really want you to succeed, because they have
something invested, as opposed to those who shout loudest). The
civic and community context looms large here. The objective should
be a nuanced institutional narrative that neither over-claims nor
under-claims, not a 'brand' which screams (Watson and Maddison
2005: ch. 6).

This is emphatically not a species of what Gordon Graham calls 'brute conservatism'; not an excuse for stasis, nor a rejection of necessary and desirable change, as the following injunctions should make clear (Graham 2005: 264). In responding to our 'true' market, I think that there are at least three areas where modern universities and their leaders need to think clearly and act positively.

The first is about adjusting and renewing the academic portfolio. Here it is important to protect the core, but also enable it to move on, chiefly through creative, temporary cross-subsidy (that is, through strategic investment in development and innovation). In psychological terms, this is very like Vygotsky's zone of 'proximal development'.

The second is about institutional status and identity. History would advise the self-confident institution not to be too precious about boundary issues. In his *The Meanings of Mass Higher Education* (1995), Peter Scott reminds the British sector that three-quarters of its universities have been founded or designated since 1945 (the proportion is even higher now), while there are no significant institutions which have not experienced merger, acquisition or loss, status change, or major changes in balance of business (Scott 1995: 44–9). Those (still) railing about the conversion of the British polytechnics and central institutions into universities in 1992 should be gently encouraged to read the extracts from the Charter of the University of Sheffield in Chapter 3.

Finally it is important to recognize that even the most powerful institution cannot really go it alone. At some stage, and for some important purposes, every institution is going to rely on the strength and reputation of the system as a whole. The dialectic between competition, collaboration, and complementarity in HE is a complex one. Mike Boxall from PA Consulting, has likened it to the *peloton* in a cycle race. This is a good metaphor. Individuals do come out of the pack, to compete for various prizes ('king of the mountains', 'points' for sprinting, and so on). There's also the *poubelle* (dustbin) bringing up the rear. But inside the *peloton* itself there is *esprit de corps* and unwritten rules (leading through your home town, assisting in re-grouping after crashes, and so on). Members of teams work for each other (including *domestiques*). Meanwhile the race remains a competition, including simply to finish: they *could* all ride slower.

Universities are extraordinarily resilient institutions; and this resilience should be used to drive change rather than defend entrenched positions. As Burton Clark concludes in his most recent book, *Sustaining Change in Universities*: 'as the twenty-first century unfolds, universities will largely get what they deserve' (Clark 2004:

184). As I have tried to suggest, merely chasing 'world-class' status may be too narrow an ambition, for individual universities and their societies. At the very least, it is not a priority likely to serve civic and community engagement.

# PART TWO: CASE STUDIES

# 5

# THE UK: THE UNIVERSITY OF BRIGHTON COMMUNITY–UNIVERSITY PARTNERSHIP PROGRAMME

*This chapter assesses the official approach to higher education community and civic engagement in the UK, especially England. It proceeds to examine a particular case study. Key themes emerging include a relatively under-developed set of national policies, coupled with institutional preoccupations (leading to a kind of fatalism) about funding. The Community–University Partnership Programme (CUPP) shows how some of the latter can be overcome.*

## The national scene

For a system that 'enjoys' the amount of surveillance that it does – from government departments and from funding councils – the 'official' line on civic and community engagement in the UK is surprisingly weak.

On the face of things, such priorities *are* recognized in public discourse. The HEFCE has added a strategic priority in its latest consultation, about 'securing the public interest' (see also Chapter 10). The formula for the third wave of Higher Education Innovation Fund (HEIF) allocations includes a modest element (up to 10 per cent) for 'engagement with non-commercial (including social and civic) organisations' (HEFCE 2005). Meanwhile, hats were tipped in this direction by both the Lambert Review (2003) and the government's response in the *Science & Innovation Investment Framework, 2004–14* (HMI/DTI/DfES 2004). 'Third leg' initiatives are all supposed to acknowledge the community interest, as in the Funding Council's Higher Education Resources for Business and Community (HEROBAC) and HEIF initiatives and the 'business and community' interaction survey. Their objective is stated as: 'to support all HE institutions in making a significant and measurable contribution to economic development and the strength of communities'. There are, however, two key sticking-points, which we in the UK have still to find our way around or through; in brutal summary these are *measurement* and *funding*, and are discussed in detail in Chapter 9.

In summary, Figure 5.1 shows how the HEFCE conceptualizes the scope of 'third-leg' initiatives. It is an ambitious and a comprehensive vision, attempting chiefly to embed higher education into the national policy frameworks with which the sector feels it should relate, especially for regional development.

*Figure 5.1* HEFCE – third stream scope

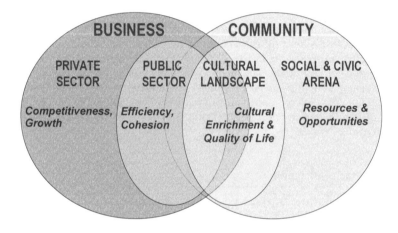

*Note:* This represents scope not scale.

*Source:* Thirunamachandran 2006

Figure 5.2 shows how related funding streams have been developed from this source, and are now planned to converge.

As for monitoring performance at the sectoral level, Table 5.1 shows the type of information about third leg performance collected by the HEFCE.

In this age of accountability, audit and atrophied trust in public institutions, it is clear that metrics and public money go together. So where else can universities and their community partners look for financial support? The resources of the community groups themselves are very limited, and likely to become more so as a result of the latest wave of central undermining of local authority finances. Both

*Figure 5.2* HEFCE – chronological funding view

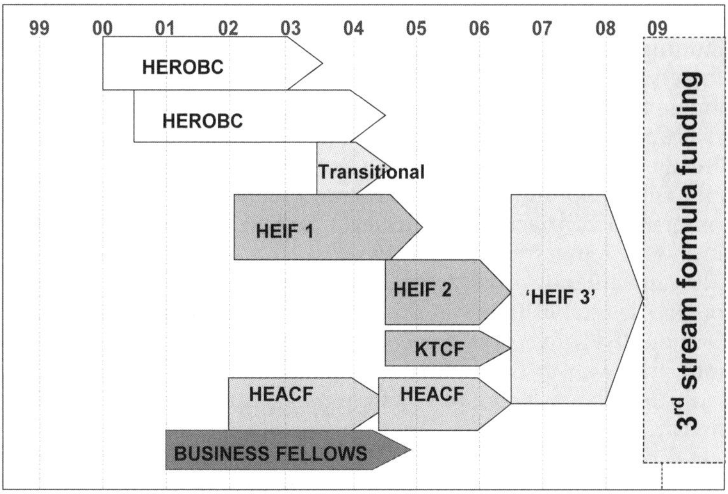

*Source:* Thirunamachandran 2006

*Table 5.1* Selected data from HE Business and Community Interaction survey (HE-BCI)

|  | 2000–01 | 2001–02 | 2002–03 | 2003–04 |
|---|---|---|---|---|
| Number of disclosures | 2,159 | 2,478 | 2,710 | 3,040 |
| Consultancy income £000s (real terms) | 103,451 | 122,155 | 168,151 | 207,831 |
| Collaborative research income £000s (real terms) | 412,380 | 469,354 | 478,573 | 541,660 |
| A required contracting system for all staff-business consulting activities (% of UK HEIs) | 60.0 | 65.2 | 66.5 | 68.3 |
| An enquiry point for SMEs (% of UK HEIs) | 83.1 | 84.8 | 89.0 | 89.6 |

*Source:* Thirunamachandran 2006

government and business contracts are now dominated by the drive for full economic costing, and no more; so the creation of 'socially useful' surpluses is less and less an option for institutions. This can also lead to a strange balance of power between the three parts of the resulting triangle. Derek Schwartz, Vice-Chancellor of Fort Hare University, described this in an extreme form in an Africa Educational Trust lecture at SOAS (10 October 2005). Because non-governmental organizations (NGOs) in South Africa are no longer directly funded, they look to the university for help. Because the university is not funded to help them, it seeks to maximize its more commercial contracts. It is, however, unable to create any serious surplus for reinvestment from these.

Private philanthropy *is* an option (for example, it played a decisive role in the establishment of the University of Brighton's pioneering Community–University Partnership Programme – see the next section), but leads to the additional strains of permanent fund-raising (with the usual concomitants of temporary staffing and permanent insecurity).

In terms of 'official' support for community engagement (broadly defined to include major initiatives such as widening participation as well as potential pump-priming for individual projects), Table 5.2 gives the view from a single HE institution (the University of Brighton) in 2004–05. Note that this summary makes no mention of funding support for individuals (hardship funds, access to learning funds, and opportunity bursaries); nor of specifically University of Brighton-style initiatives (like relevant projects of the Community–University Partnership Programme, or the HEIF-funded Community Knowledge Exchange – jointly funded with the University of Sussex). Similar 'maps' could be constructed from the point of view of a further education institution (FEI), a local authority, or even broader constituencies such as students. The key point is the complexity of the streams that have to be managed, each with its own time-scale and framework for accountability.

## The Community–University Partnership Programme

The University of Brighton has the sort of rich, community-orientated history enjoyed by many of the UK's former polytechnics. Essentially it has grown as a federation of professional schools, each locally supported (and often funded by the community) at different stages in its history: art, design and crafts (including construction) in the mid-nineteenth century, science and technology at the turn of the twentieth century, teacher education throughout the twentieth

*Table 5.2* HEFCE support for community initiatives, 2004–05

| Name of initiative/project | Funder(s)/ sponsor(s) | Time line | Funding £ (per year) |
|---|---|---|---|
| Special initiatives to encourage WP in HE of students with special needs | HEFCE | Piloted 1993–94 Roll out 1994–95 | Nationally: £3m Per project: £10k |
| HEFCE Formula Funds | HEFCE | 1999 to date (although formula methodology has changed over this period) | UoB: approx. £335k p.a. for widening access and £130k for disability |
| HEFCE Special Initiative funding (funding for Sussex Coastal Highway, now migrated into Aimhigher) | HEFCE | 1999 to 2002 | Sussex partnership £410k over 3 years |
| HEFCE Summer Schools (now match funding through ESF* to allow expansion of scheme) | HEFCE (ESF from 2003–4) | 2001 to date | Nationally £10m UoB: approx. £43k p.a. |
| Education Action Zones/ Excellence in Cities (now merged with Aimhigher) | DfES | 1998 to 2003 (merged with Aimhigher in 2003–04 | Approx. £55m from DfES Approx. £37m from private business |
| Aspiration funding (for 'worst performing institutions in respect to WP') | HEFCE | 2000–01 to 2003–04 | £6m annually |
| Higher Education Innovation Fund 2 (Community Knowledge Exchange bid) | HEFCE | HEIF 2 2004–05 to 2006–07 | Nationally: £10m. UoB partnership £370k |
| Active Community Fund (student volunteering) | HEFCE | Round 1: 2001– 02 to 2003–04 | Nationally: Round 1 = £27m |

| Name of initiative/project | Funder(s)/ sponsor(s) | Time line | Funding £ (per year) |
|---|---|---|---|
| | | | Round 2 = £10m |
| | | Round 2: 2004–05 to 2005–06 continuation funding | UoB: Round 1: 2001–04 £279k Round 2: 2004– 06 (continuation funding) £101k |

*Note:* * European Social Fund.

*Source:* Watson 2005a

century, and more recently health and medicine including the early twenty-first-century foundation of a medical school (jointly with the University of Sussex). The institution today has an enviable national (and in some fields international) reputation, but its strategic development is still heavily influenced by a sense of responsibility to the community. For example, two of the six themes in the current (2002–07) corporate plan, are as follows:

- the university will continue to collaborate actively with selected local, national and international partners on the basis of mutual respect; and
- the university will further improve the environment in which members of its community study, work and live, and will contribute positively to the wider environment (Watson and Maddison 2005: 28–9, 99).

The Community–University Partnership Programme, which began in 2003, is an example of how these more generalized intentions can be catalysed (for more detail see www.cupp.org.uk). The main distinctive features of the CUPP project are:

- the vital enabling role played by an initial philanthropic donation (from the Atlantic Philanthropies);
- the strategic decision to embed projects in academic schools and departments, and hence connect to core business;

- an emphasis on knowledge exchange, rather than linear knowledge transfer (KT);
- the ambition to extend student learning in the community;
- the 'leverage' of CUPP resources into other HEFCE programmes (notably HEIF);
- the reliance on partnership with other organizations, including other HEIs; and
- the innovation of the research help-desk.

There follows some personal testimony about the origins and objectives of the Programme, taken from a film – *In It Together: The Community–University Partnership Programme* – produced in 2006.

> The history is quite interesting. It begins when I appeared on a Radio 4 programme called '*The Commission*', which you might know, and we recorded a programme about whether the expansion of higher education had been a good thing or a bad thing. The great and the good were wheeled out to quiz me about whether we needed more graduates or plumbers. I made a number of points on that programme about the democratic advantages of widening participation. Following that I was actually contacted by a representative of our major funder for this project, who asked me if there was any way in which he and his organization could help. I think that there was a sense that Brighton was making a case for growing out of the community. And for giving a lot back to the community, and he was interested in pursuing that. That's the germ from which the notion of the Community–University Partnership Project grew. It drew together some things that the university was doing already, but it had an extra layer of external support, which enabled us to move into some new, more experimental areas, and the results are, I think beginning to bear fruit.
>
> What makes CUPP particularly interesting is the nature of the dialogue between the community and the university that leads to the projects. We have created a space where our expertise, their needs, and also their expertise in many instances can come together.
>
> (David Watson, Vice-Chancellor,
> University of Brighton, 1990–2005)

It's been a commonplace that universities have helped commercial organizations and businesses to innovate and to research and to develop themselves in all sorts of ways, and there has been a lot of attention placed on that, but in the main there has been little activity that has linked the expertise, resources and facilities that are located with higher education and directed them towards social problems within local communities. There have been bits and pieces; there has been sporadic activity within a number of notable schemes, but I think what is different about the Community–University Partnership Programme at Brighton University is that it attempts to link the whole of the university and its expertise and resources with its local community. It's a strategic project.

(David Wolff, Director of CUPP)

We do a lot of things to serve the needs of the economy by working with businesses; we do a lot of things to produce the surveyors, the architects, the teachers, the designers, the doctors – all of those things which we all need; and that's our job, and we are proud to do it and think it's very important. But also part of our job is to help build and sustain people's ideas about citizenship; their ideas about how to work together in communities – providing them with the resources to do that, to support ideas about environmental policies, about equalities, about communities working together, about arts, about art and architecture existing within people's lives – for enjoyment, for fulfilment, to help them create and develop. I think the rounded picture should have all of those things in mind and see them all together, and I think the CUPP project has enabled us to fill in another bit of that picture, which is often harder to fill because – for better or worse – current streams of public funding tend to favour things where the economic benefit is seen to be more immediate.

(Stuart Laing, Pro-Vice-Chancellor (Academic Affairs))

Well, I happen to believe that universities are 'think tanks', where people sit in a very privileged position, and are paid to think. Now that's great, and I've done that all my life. But they also have a duty: a duty of care, in my view, to the surrounding areas, and certainly a duty of analysis. So we are paid, in a sense, to look at the situation, and say what has gone wrong, and, if possible, to induce people to think about what has gone wrong, and then induce them (because it is affecting them) to develop ways by which they can begin to redress the situation

themselves. And I think CUPP-type activities, in terms of empowering people, in terms of giving people access to education,
adult learning, to leisure facilities and so on, which they would
not previously have had without a special programme, is all part
of that. Now, it's not enormous. I think one has to say that there
need to be CUPPs all round the country, in order to have a
quantum effect on this situation.

(Peter Ambrose, Visiting Professor in the
Heath and Social Policy Research Centre)

The CUPP works with a number of community organizations in
the Brighton and Sussex locality as well as with the University of
Sussex (chiefly through the Brighton and Sussex Community
Knowledge Exchange – BSCKE). The BSCKE is a particularly innovative device, using HEIF money to apply the highly successful
'teaching Company' (now Knowledge-Transfer Partnership) model to
the community sector. This involves supporting a postgraduate
'associate' within the organization, jointly supervised by the university and the 'company', working on a project that can also have
an academic outcome such as a postgraduate thesis. The CUPP
steering group includes members from the university and community sectors. Within the university, academics are involved from
across the subject range. Within the community, the emphasis has
been on working with disadvantaged groups in order to support social and economic inclusion.

Specific examples of local populations involved in CUPP and
BSCKE activities include the local refugee communities; groups of
adults with learning disabilities; parents/carers of vulnerable children; and the local lesbian, gay, bisexual and transgender population. The nature of involvement can vary from a telephone
conversation with the research help-desk through to a fully fledged
BSCKE project funded at £25k. 'Live' projects supported in whole or
in part through the CUPP and the BSCKE include the following:

- Football 4 Unity (F4U) – addressing social inclusion and commu-
  nity relations through sport (which draws on the well-established
  Brighton-led F4P – Football for Peace – project, an annual event in
  Northern Israel, between Jewish and Arab communities);
- Box of Tricks – ordinary magic that helps build resilience in dis-
  advantaged children (based on a therapeutic methodology called
  Resilent Therapy – RT);
- Aspire – identifying barriers that prevent people with Asperger's
  Syndrome getting into work;

- Hear Our Voices – putting domestic violence survivors at the heart of informing service delivery;
- the needs of homeless lesbian, gay and transgender young people;
- Refugees in research – finding new voices;
- Refugee Education Mentoring Advice and Support into Higher Education (REMAS HE);
- Access to Art – one of the CUPP's pioneering projects, now moving into a new phase in Hastings;
- Wellbeing, Health and Occupation for Older People (WHOOP);
- evaluating extended services at Falmer High School;
- six connected projects evaluating local organizations working on neighbourhood renewal;
- promoting the exchange of knowledge and evidence among those working on substance misuse;
- Tec-Cement – the School of the Environment working with the Low Carbon Network to develop the use of recycled materials in aggregate mix;
- Open Architecture – a studio for all final year students which involves direct work on community projects; and
- Assisting sustainable development – a project supporting Neighbourhood Action on Climate Change.

As this partial list confirms, CUPP projects now draw upon the full range of disciplinary resources of the university and nearly all include a specific research base. In this sense they demonstrate specific 'added value' from the HEI's intellectual capital, and satisfy the 'audit trail' back to core business discussed in Chapter 9.

Outcomes are of six main kinds:

- individual projects, each of which includes a formal evaluation. Here the outcomes can be a written report (for example, where the project has focused on an evaluation of community activity) or an artefact (for example, the pieces made by artists with learning disabilities or the structures made by architecture students working with disadvantaged community groups);
- contributions to the university's 'core business' of learning, teaching and research. Examples include the development of a new course module enabling students involved in CUPP-type activities to gain academic credit for their involvement, a new pathway in the university's suite of Masters degrees, and work with the University of Sussex to create a new Foundation Degree in Community Service;
- enhancement of the University's capacity to engage in community-based activities. As well as supporting a range of individual

projects, and leveraging other funding into community engagement activity, the CUPP has become a gateway into the university for the community and voluntary sectors, strengthening the dialogue and providing a focal point for conversation and more general collaboration. The university's local reputation has been enhanced as a result;

- increase in the community and voluntary sector's capacity. It is clear that the CUPP, chiefly perhaps through the research help-desk and by partnering other funding proposals, is starting to have an impact on the way in which local organizations are able to work, including greater self-confidence in using evidence in funding proposals, wider influence, and improved service delivery;
- evidence of improved sustainability of projects, including through follow-on funding; and
- contributions to the wider policy debate. Here the impact remains to be fully assessed, but the CUPP – and the university – have been keen to ensure that it also seeks to influence the development of thinking about 'third stream' funding and the role of universities. This has included taking part in work with HEFCE on metrics by which future funding might be driven (as discussed in Chapter 9).

As for 'measurement', some of the 'metrics' for the CUPP and the BSCKE include the following:

- a high level of demand for the research help-desk – over 200 enquiries in year one;
- a launch event attended by nearly 100 people in March 2004;
- an international conference on 'community–university partnerships for community–university benefits' held in April 2006 (see CUPP 2006);
- development of a range of help-desk services from drop-in sessions to formal training events;
- referral of community groups to schools for projects involving student volunteers;
- leveraging of additional funding of over £430k in year one; and
- production of two short films: one about the 'Access to Arts' project, as well as *In It Together*.

The initial grant runs from 2003 to 2007. The main lessons to date have to do with capacity; the ability of the university to respond to an approach from a community organization or to develop an idea into a project is limited by resources – there is no shortage of projects.

Securing time from leading academics has been crucial. This has been done by 'buying' some of their time with a cash payment to their school (where the value of the time delivered invariably exceeds the cash transfer). Where this has not been done, it has been much harder for individuals to take part at any serious level. The CUPP has a vital matching or brokering role to explore the best way in which the university's assets can be developed in this way. In doing so it has captured the existing enthusiasm and commitment of a number of academics and enabled them to channel their interests and expertise by providing a point of contact with external organizations. Sustainability appears most likely where engagement activity (for example, from a small-scale project) can become part of the university's core business, whether undergraduate or postgraduate learning and teaching or research. There can be genuine exchange and partnership, where the university and community both learn and benefit. Positive results like this depend upon support and a preparedness to learn (for example, about differences in language and culture) and do not happen accidentally. The BSCKE has as one of its core activities a forum intended to support learning between projects as well as to draw in individuals not currently working on projects but interested in the general ideas.

As Angie Hart and David Wollf have reflected in an early account of the experience of the CUPP, the importance of engagement up and down the university is at least as important as the relationships established between the university and its partners. For example, leadership rhetoric at one end of the spectrum and student enthusiasm for volunteering at the other will remain unconnected, unless the detailed, positive engagement of academics and support staff can be secured at departmental level. Their tips are as follows:

- establish a language that you can all use to talk about processes and structures;
- work with those who want to work with you;
- secure funds to buy academics and practitioners out;
- strategically set up links that go with the strengths of the university;
- emphasize 'practice' rather than organizational form or structure;
- take spatial issues seriously (they focus particularly on how community partners are welcomed into the 'spaces' of the university, such as libraries and recreational facilities);
- do not let definitional problems stop you in your tracks;
- emphasize the positive;
- use community–university brokers who can work across different cultures and in different languages;
- enjoy the relationships; and
- find creative ways around the normal university process as what

you need to do will often not fit the standard mould (Hart and Wolff 2006: 135–6).

There is a standard trajectory for the development of several elements of the work. One example concerns work with the parents/carers of parents of children with disabilities. Here, an initial enquiry to the help-desk moved through attendance at a workshop and one-to-one conversation with an academic into a major project securing external funding of over £100k. The quality of the individuals involved from the university is key, and this applies to the administrative staff leading the CUPP as well as the academics with whom they work. Senior leadership commitment has been important, including ensuring that the Board of Governors and external stakeholders are well informed about progress, success and impact.

The main challenges are those of scale and sustainability – and these dimensions have a financial and an academic component. International collaborators with whom the CUPP has worked suggest that initiatives of this kind take ten years to become fully established. The CUPP is in its early years, so its managers are aware that there is much to do to establish the 'right size' for the CUPP as well as to enable it to become even more part of mainstream university activity. The latter will involve working out the best ways, in terms of people, processes and structures, to relate CUPP-type work to other activities of the 'third stream' and outreach aimed at widening participation.

Taking the financial component of the challenge first, the set-up funding from the charitable foundation will expire in 2007 and the foundation has confirmed that its funding priorities have changed such that it will not consider further funding for the CUPP. The university has meanwhile established a basic level of funding for the work to continue, although fund-raising will remain important. Turning to the academic component, key members of staff are optimistic about the academic sustainability provided they can continue to succeed in identifying a relationship between CUPP-sponsored activity and 'core business' of learning, teaching and research.

# 6

# AUSTRALIA: THE UNIVERSITY OF QUEENSLAND BOILERHOUSE PROJECT

*Universities in Australia have demonstrated a strong commitment to collective action, and to drawing state, local and national governments into the higher education civic agenda. This chapter describes aspects of the national history, as well as a case study involving significant upfront investment by a leading research-intensive university (the University of Queensland), and the range of projects and relationships which emerge.*

## The national scene

Australia has developed its commitment to university civic engagement recently but rapidly, as evidenced by the strength of the Australian Consortium on Higher Education, Community Engagement and Social Responsibility (see their foundation paper in Sunderland *et al.* 2004). A new national alliance – the Australian Universities Community Engagement Alliance Inc. (AUCEA) – was incorporated in 2004 under the leadership of the University of Western Sydney, and currently has 25 institutional members. It also has formal support from the federal Department of Education, Science and Training (DEST), sponsors annual national conferences, and has established an online refereed journal, the *Australasian Journal of Community Engagement*. (See www.aucea.net.au.)

More analytically, Winter, Wiseman and Muirhead have attempted an audit of how the nine, very different universities in the State of Victoria have addressed the civic agenda (Winter *et al.* forthcoming). The main conclusion concerns the convergence between university strategies and political preferences in early twenty-first-century social policy. In the course of a subtle analysis, they find traditional ideals of social 'service' by universities having been superseded by a strong construction of the 'community', the latter structured particularly around economic rationalism. Thus 'new public management' is shown to straddle the boundary between the university and the communities it serves. In summary, a notion of the civic role of universities as a 'strategy of resistance' has been superseded by a set of obligations to the community organized around specific, often government-led, interventions.

At the same time, there are particular Australian concern which resonate throughout this domain. One is rural deprivation. The vast majority of Australians live and work in cities, and so it is the 'last resort' public services which keep rural needs on the agenda; and higher education has woken up to its responsibilities within this context. Two issues almost immediately arise: responsibilities to the indigeneous population (shared with universities in New Zealand, South Africa and Canada, although interestingly hardly at all in the USA) and water (as in the Middle East).

Otherwise, concerns are familiar: a regret about the 'depoliticisation of the student body' (potentially exacerbated by the Howard government's forcing through of its Voluntary Student Unionism bill); a tendency for the higher status institutions (notably the University of Melbourne) to hold the strongest sense of a transnational constituency (the others claim a far stronger sense of local and regional 'place'); and uneasiness about increasing student instrumentalism. (For a valuable survey of these and other related developments at the national level, see Marginson 1997: *passim*.)

Laurence Brown and Bruce Muirhead have set some of these tensions and anxieties within a broader frame:

> The current 'rush to community' being displayed by the universities suggests that the cultural revolutions wrought by the changes in university profile and population of the 40s through the 70s and the funding cuts and corporate culture of the universities in the 80s and 90s has practically forced an opportunity to come to terms with the university's natural constituency: the local community ... In a very real sense, engagement with local communities can effect a re-humanization and a renewal of the university as global (truth), national (productive) and communal (civic). If we do not take the chance to re-evaluate the civic mission of the university in this country we will have squandered an opportunity to revitalize and re-apply the medieval concept of the university in Australia's modern and more egalitarian society.
>
> (Brown and Muirhead 2001: 15)

## The Boilerhouse

In this national development, a clear lead has been taken by the University of Queensland (UQ), not least by developments on its pioneering Ipswich campus. The following account, by Bruce Muirhead, its first director, shows where the Boilerhouse came from, and why it has succeeded in capturing the imagination of many of those who work with it.

In early 1999, an elderly Ipswich resident was assaulted on the street. He died from his injuries. The local community was very concerned that such a fate should befall a vulnerable person, seemingly at the hands of a group of seven young people within the care of various Government agencies. This incident was one of a number of significant issues that had troubled the Ipswich community over an extended period of time.

Over the following five years, local community, government and academic leaders confronted the issue of how to get government departments and communities working together so that tragedies like this would not recur. Results included a series of accredited and short course in community and interprofessional leadership, developed locally and collaboratively between Ipswich community and the UQ 'Boilerhouse' Centre.

Since then, more than 200 community leaders have completed this training. They include young parents from Riverview, current and retired mayors, regional managers of government, school principals and teachers. More than $1 million was raised for community-based collaborative research involving everyone from grandmothers to young people and cultural leaders.

Ultimately, these courses and research programs have changed the lives of individuals and organizations and influenced the city's plans for future development.

The Centre provided leadership for this group of senior regional managers by facilitating discussions and connections with other agencies. Over a period of twelve months, fortnightly breakfast meetings were held. The numbers of senior executives attending these meetings increased from 3 to 20. Consistent themes began to emerge from these discussions: the need to focus on building community capability; the need for a holistic collaborative effort across all levels; difficulties in operating effectively with government programs organized around 'silos'; government programs having difficulty pooling resources and working collaboratively to address identified

> regional problems; and goodwill between agencies to address
> these issues.
>
> (Personal communication)

The result was the UQ Community Service and Research Centre, a flagship enterprise for the new campus, based on the elegantly refurbished site of a former mental hospital, in the heart of a community dogged by economic deprivation and political extremism (it includes the constituency of the former 'Australia First' Senator Pauline Hanson). The Boilerhouse goal is 'to facilitate just and sustainable community outcomes', through an emphatically collaborative approach: collaboration 'opens up new possibilities for innovation – responsibility is shared, diverse perspectives are heard and resources can be used more effectively'. In other words, the Boilerhouse sets out to be exactly the sort of 'borderland' institution discussed in Chapter 9, specifically located between and including the university and its community. The resulting principles and commitments include those of:

- collaborative responses to local issues;
- active citizenship;
- personal relationships as a basis for collaboration; and
- sustainable development, incorporating a balance between social justice, economic stability and equity, environmental protection, and participatory governance (see www.uq.edu.au/boilerhouse/).

At the time of writing, the centre is embarking on its second five-year plan, under new leadership. Its priorities reflect some of the themes set out above: a strong theoretical commitment to building social capital; particular attention to rural economic development and to culturally and linguistically diverse groups (CaLD), as well to Australia's ageing population; and contributions to community capacity building and to service integration. Specific projects include 'developing a collaborative approach to ageing well in the community'; providing an 'integrated social planning and infrastructure assessment' for the many initiatives under way in South East Queensland'; and a series of access and social equity initiatives for students from CaLD communities in the Ipswich/Inala corridor.

Meanwhile Muirhead has moved on to head Eidos, an organization dedicated to harness the learning power of universities and their partners on a wider scale.

# 7

# THE USA: THE UNIVERSITY OF PENNSYLVANIA CENTER FOR COMMUNITY PARTNERSHIPS

*The USA's higher education system is frequently characterized as the most market orientated in the world. This has an effect on civic and community engagement, as mission differentiation and strategic choice is apparently much less trammelled than elsewhere. This chapter describes the range – of institutional types as well as of curriculum option – and shows the impact of choices made by a leading research university.*

## The national scene

In contrast to both the UK and Australia, the USA has a much more variegated and diverse higher education system, with consequently a broad spectrum of types of relationship with the community and with local and state authorities. At one end of the spectrum is the huge community college network, as its title implies, intimately related with both local economies and political preferences. At the other there is the pinnacle of private, research-intensive universities, often having fraught and tense relationships with their immediate localities. Several of these could indeed be described as 'castles in the swamp'.

Meanwhile, the USA could be said to have led the world in developing powerful models of how universities and colleges can relate to their communities: these range from strong commitments to service learning and for academic credit for positive action by students within the community to internationally leading business and other professional schools who share in the development of economic policy and delivery of professional services (see Maurrasse 2001: 11–28). There have also been high-profile examples of collective approaches to university–community interaction such as Campus Compact, with nearly 1000 college Presidents as signatories (Musil 2003; Arthur with Bohlin 2005: 60–1). The Association of American Colleges and Universities (AAC&U) has established a Center for Liberal Education and Civic Engagement and called for a new understanding of 'civic learning' (see www.aacu.org/civic_engagement).

Three other elements stand out in any account of how university communities in the USA can energize particularly undergraduates and their teachers. The first is the presence of many mission-specific, often faith-based institutions, which see 'service' as a prime strategic goal (see Annette in Arthur with Bohlin 2005: 57–60).

The second is a concept of 'active citizenship', which sees political engagement as a worthy and non-contentious outcome (in this the US participants in initiatives like the 'Wingspread Declaration on Renewing the Civic Mission of the American Research University' have less compunction about joining political debate about the future of their society than their counterparts in Europe and Australasia) (see Arthur with Bohlin 2005: 83). It is perhaps indicative that American HEIs in receipt of federal funds are required to distribute voter-registration forms to their students. Nor are such drivers confined to the domestic arena. Tufts University recently announced that it would use a $100 million gift (the largest in its history) to set up a micro-loan system for the developing world, involving students in the investment decisions (Fain 2005b). More broadly, Tufts is not only responsible for the Talloires initiative (described in the Introduction) but has sought to establish 'civic engagement as a Tufts signature' (Ostrander 2006; see also Gittleman 2004).

The third is a practical point about the undergraduate curriculum. In the USA it is rarely utilized as a means of professional formation, as it is frequently elsewhere in the world (most formal 'licensing' activity starts at the postgraduate level). As a consequence, there is considerably more freedom to use credit-bearing time on a course in community-based activity, including service learning. Derek Bok estimates that 'almost half of all students in four-year colleges now spend time volunteering'. He is, however, conscious that, in the context of the party-political definition of 'active citizenship', such activity can act as displacement (although probably not nearly as much as in the UK): community service can be seen 'as an *alternative* to politics and government' (Bok 2006: 180, 183; original emphasis).

## The Center for Community Partnerships

The University of Pennsylvania has to be the brand leader for the USA's commitment to university civic and community engagement. The university itself is a highly aspirant member of the Ivy League, proud of its rising position in *US News and World Report*'s league table (at the time of writing it is fourth). However, it is also acutely conscious of its development immediately adjacent to a particularly deprived part of West Philadelphia, contiguous with what is called, without irony 'University City'. The extended neighbourhood of Western Philadelphia continues to see middle-class flight, higher than average unemployment, and an increase in the number of families below the poverty line (Fain 2005a).

Throughout the 1990s the university attempted to tackle many of the resulting isssues head-on, not least by the creation of the Center for Community Partnerships (CCP) in 1992 (Maurrasse 2001: 29–64). The CCP, led from its inception by Penn history graduate Ira Harkavy, has captured the interest of communities both inside and outside the university. Perhaps most notably it has established itself as a nett contributor to the university's own intellectual capital (principally as marshalled by Penn's Professor Lee Benson) and won consistent presidential support. Benson and Harkavy set the tone with an initiative derived from an honours undergraduate history seminar on university–community relationships, first taught by both of them in 1985: the West Philadelphia Improvement Corps (WEPIC). This established perhaps the strongest theme in the Penn community engagement portfolio (and the one most intensively replicated elsewhere): the development of university-assisted community schools. Together Harkavay and Benson built a network of support, commitment and intellectual interest across the university and out into the community. Support from the university's presidents was notable. The seminar was also contributed to President Sheldon Hackney, himself a historian and later President of the National Endowment for the Humanities (NEH). Within a short time it came to be known as 'the President's seminar'. More recently the mantle has been taken up by Penn's current president, Amy Guttman, author of works like *Democratic Education* (1987). There is a strong philosophical commitment underlying this work, derived from John Dewey's twin notions of active learning and participatory democracy (see Harkavy and Benson 1998).

This is how Harkavy describes the CCP and its goals:

> The Center for Community Partnerships is engaged in an innovative effort to connect the academic mission of the University

with the aspirations of its community. This is a great change. For most of its history Penn was in but not of its community. Emerging from the Second World War as a quiet regional school with a large number of commuting students, the University began to attract government attention and research money. Ideally placed in a major eastern city and surrounded by its rich resources, Penn began to grow and expand its urban campus, often without considering the consequences for its neighbors.

In the last several decades of the twentieth century, Penn emerged as a pre-eminent research university, ranked in the top ten in the country. As the University flourished, much of West Philadelphia declined, losing economic and social capital.

Many people, however, were coming to realize that the futures of Penn and West Philadelphia were intertwined. Beginning in the 1980s, serious attention began to be focused on how Penn could help play an active, collaborative role creating partnerships with the key strategic community institutions – schools, neighborhood organizations, and communities of faith – to effect positive change.

(Personal communication)

The results keep Penn comfortably at the head of national accounts of both service learning and community engagement. In 2004–05 the CCP was able to report 62 academically-based community service courses taught across 19 departments and 8 schools (including 16 graduate courses). In the same year, 1650 students earned credit in this way and over 60 faculty were directly involved (Weeks 2006). And much of the activity is very highly focused; Penn wins particular plaudits for its pioneering Urban Nutrition Initiative (UNI), which runs the gamut from school gardens and meals plans, through nutrition-monitoring and health interventions, to direct advocacy and lobbying with city and local government. The 'gap', acknowledged by all of the key players as a priority for attention (although very hard to tackle), is the tiny number of young West Philadelphia residents who are able to enrol at Penn (Maurrasse 2001: 183).

On a wider scale Penn coordinates a higher education network for neighbourhood development within the city (with 42 partners), a state-wide service-learning alliance, a 'replication project' which seeks to roll-out its community-school programme in other locations (currently 23) and is the organizational centre for the International Consortium for Higher Education, Civic Responsibility and Democracy (as described in the Introduction to this book – Chapter 1) (Weeks 2006).

# 8

# GLOBAL BENCHMARKING: THE ASSOCIATION OF COMMONWEALTH UNIVERSITIES

*In 2004 the author was contracted by the ACU to develop and operate an international benchmarking tool for universities' civic engagement. This chapter outlines:*

- *the scheme;*
- *the anonymized results (which came from universities in Australia, Canada, New Zealand, Southern Africa, the UK, and the West Indies); and*
- *conclusions in the form of a core agenda for universities wishing to enhance their civic engagement.*

*It concludes with some alternative approaches to relevant institutional self-study and both international and inter-institutional benchmarking.*

## The ACU scheme

Participating institutions in the ACU benchmarking exercise on 'managing civic engagement' (held in Perth in August 2004) were asked to respond to a questionnaire, on the basis of addressing five issues:

(a) clarifying the university's historical and mission-based commitments to its host society;
(b) identifying how engagement informs and influences the university's range of operations;
(c) describing how the university is organized to meet the challenge of civic engagement;

(d) assessing the contribution of staff, students and external partners to the engagement agenda; and

(e) monitoring achievements, constraints and future opportunities for civic engagement.

This schema has also been adopted for use by the Talloires group.

*1. Mission and history*

Participants were asked to describe how the origins and development of their universities incorporate commitments to the development of the region and locality.

1.1 What relevant objectives are set for the institution in its founding document (charter or equivalent)?

1.2 What relevant expectations are held by those who fund your work and support it (including politically)?

1.3 Which external groups are represented *ex officio* and *de facto* on the university's governance or senior management bodies? How are the relevant individuals chosen and how do they see their roles?

1.4 To whom does the university regard itself as accountable for its civic mission? For example, is there a 'stakeholder group' such as a university Court, and if so, how does this work?

1.5 Are 'engagement' objectives (as defined above) specified in the university's strategic plan? If so, how, and with what indicators of success?

1.6 Have changes over time in the university's composition or status (e.g. mergers, acquisitions, large scale contracts) affected the engagement agenda? If so, in what manner?

*2. Balance of activities*

Participants were asked to describe how the university's pattern of activities reflects a civic engagement agenda.

2.1 Give a brief assessment of the chief economic and social needs of your region and/or locality. Include a description of the main sources of this information.

2.2 How does the university's *teaching* profile (by subject and level, and including continuous professional development [CPD] and lifelong learning) reflect the needs of the local community and region? To what extent does the curriculum incorporate relevant features of the following:

(a)    structured and assessed work experience and/or work-based learning;
(b)    'service learning'; and/or
(c)    prior or concurrent informal work experience?

2.2.1 How can representatives of the local and regional economy and community influence curriculum and other choices?

2.3 What proportion of the university's *research* activity is directed towards the needs of the local and regional economy and society?

2.3.1 How can representatives of the local and regional economy and community influence research priorities?

2.4 How would the university describe its *service* objectives (i.e. its commitments to business and the community)?

2.4.1 How can representatives of the local and regional economy and community influence activities in this area?

2.5 Using as a proxy an estimate of staff time (academic and support), how far is engagement in each of the areas outlined in this section (teaching, research and service) directed towards:

(a)    large business and industrial interests (including global and national organisations present in the region);
(b)    small and medium-sized enterprises;
(c)    other public services (e.g. education, health, social services);
(d)    the voluntary sector, community groups and NGOs; and
(e)    cultural and artistic organisations?

[It was suggested that a matrix, summing to 100% as the total staff effort involved in civic engagement, would be helpful.]

2.6 Does the university have any other policies (e.g. on environmental responsibility, equality of opportunity, recruitment, procurement of goods and services) which can act positively or negatively on the region and the locality?

*3. Organisation*

Participants were asked to describe how their universities organised themselves and deployed their resources (including human resources) to meet civic objectives.

3.1 Does the university have specialised services to meet civic and related objectives (e.g. web-based resources, business advisory services, help-desks, formal consultancy and related services)?

3.1.1 If so, do these operate at a central or a devolved level, and if both how do the levels relate?

3.2 Does the university have either dedicated or shared services which are community-facing (such as libraries, performance or exhibition spaces, sports facilities)?

3.3 On what terms and with what frequency and volume of uptake are the university's campus or campuses accessible to the community?

3.4 What arrangements are made for the security of the members, guests, and property of the university?

*4. People*

Participants were asked to describe how policies and practice involve members of the university including staff and various levels, students and formal partners in achieving goals related to civic engagement.

4.1 Who takes primary responsibility for the university's work in civic engagement as defined in response to question 1.5 (above)?

4.2 Does the university's policy for student recruitment have a local or a regional dimension? If so, how is this determined and what impact does it have on the make-up of the university community?

4.3 To what extent are civic engagement objectives built into contractual terms for:

(a)    senior managers;

(b)    academic staff; and

(c)    support staff (including the specialised staff referred to in question 3.1 above)?

4.3.1 Can achievement against such objectives positively influence decisions on promotion and re-grading?

4.4 Reflecting on the answer to question 2.2 (above), how far is the student body engaged in the economic and cultural life of the community through formal requirements?

4.5 What proportion of the student body (for example, post-graduate or post-experience students) is concurrently in full-time local or regionally-based employment?

4.6 What encouragement is there for members of staff to undertake aspects of community service (e.g. service on boards of other organisations, *pro bono* advice, elected political office)?

4.7 What is the extent of student volunteering in the community, and how is this organised? Does it attract:

(a)  formal support (e.g. timetable concessions, payment of expenses); and/or

(b)  academic credit?

*5. Monitoring, evaluation and communication*

Participants were asked to describe how their universities set objectives and targets for civic engagement, monitor and evaluate achievement, and communicate both their intentions and related activities.

5.1 Has the university undertaken any survey research to test either internal and/or external interest in and proposals for the civic engagement agenda? If so, please summarise the results.
5.2 What steps does the university take to consult upon and publicise its civic engagement agenda? [It may be helpful to review such publications as annual reports, newsletters and alumni communications.]
5.3 What do you regard as the level of public confidence held at national, regional and local level in the overall performance of your university? What steps can be taken either to maintain or improve this level?

*6. Coda*

6.1 Reflecting on the answer to question 1.5 above, participants were asked to identify up to five significant achievements and up to five unmet ambitions demonstrated by the university at present. Both qualitative and quantitative descriptions would be welcome.

## Responses

The exercise revealed some of the weaknesses as well as the basic utility of the assessment template. As an abstract preliminary analytical framework, this was necessarily something of a counsel of perfection. No institution could expect to be persuasive against each challenge or in every detail. Indeed, the responses were appropriately self-confident and self-critical. On balance, universities found it easier to record aspirations and broad strategic goals than targets and their effective monitoring. They were honest about both the external and internal inhibitions constraining this aspect of institutional performance.

They also recorded in rich detail some of the things that work and some of the plans which were about to come to fruition. Many of these are recorded – although in necessarily rather abstract terms – in a 'composite' statement of good practice (subsequently refined and circulated to the group). The prospects for creative sharing of experience were good.

At the more strategic level, a number of potential topics for discussion emerged immediately from the comparative study.

## History and reality

The circumstances of the foundation of individual institutions, and of their resulting legal and governance frameworks were dominant. These range from conditions in which the university is directly tied to state or regional government priorities, through those where 'State Partnership' agreements have been struck, to those where autonomy and independence are regarded as overriding values. One university had as its goal the 'political transformation' of the society it serves.

Most of the universities taking part had gone through significant phases of institutional development, often beginning with highly specific professional and vocational objectives (characteristically at the turn of the twentieth century) and subsequently taking on more general university objectives including wider curricula and research (characteristically through late twentieth-century reforms of national systems).

At a more mundane level, interventions undertaken by some respondents would be culturally unacceptable, or even illegal in other respondents' operating context (an example of the latter is regional or local preference for procurement of goods and services).

## Defining community

The exercise opened up a set of key definitional questions. As one respondent underlined, universities arguably serve multiple communities, of which one is the voluntary academic community itself. Meanwhile, are universities responsible to civil society or to nations (see the discussion in Chapters 10 and 11)? One respondent emphasized how in its case the 'community is the nation'. Another argued strongly for the mutual dependence of local and global priorities in its strategy.

Then there were important questions about multiculturalism, of language and cultural inheritance, and of 'first nations' and aboriginal responsibilities.

Another set of definitional issues was raised by the perception and analysis of 'stakeholders', a concept appealed to by almost all of the respondents (again see Chapter 11 for further discussion of this concept).

## The terms of trade

### 1. *Dialogue between the university and the community*

In most cases evidence of 'out-reach' trumped evidence of 'outside-in' influence. The balance between the university declaring what services it offers (and acting to make those available) on the one hand, and the community directly influencing the programme of work of the university (including by establishing priorities which the latter might not prefer) was at least superficially uneven. Some of the most eloquent examples of this dilemma occurred when the two sides managed to construct a 'neutral' ground on which to explore the issues.

### 2. *Competition, collaboration and complementarity*

Partnerships and mutual planning contended in many cases with markets and state-imposed entrepreneurialism. Several submissions revealed the tension between responding constructively to political and other external pressures, and having to cope with competition from other institutions.

## The challenge of self-study

Community and civic engagement was argued for in all cases on an ethical and value basis. In this sense it often reversed the priorities of funders, as well as of business and political leaders who emphasize the direct and indirect economic impact of effective higher education. Truly understanding outcomes and impact in both of these areas was seen as a serious challenge.

*Figure 8.1*   The ACU 'composite'

1. Mission includes local/regional community support
2. Structured/comprehensive external advice on curriculum
3. Widespread student placements/assessed work experience
4. Shared facilities/regular public events
5. Structured business advice services and delivery, including for voluntary sector
6. Outreach incentives for staff
7. Regular public events
8. Regional public service/local authority contracts
9. Formal contributions to local schools
10. Industry clubs or equivalent
11. Supported student volunteering
12. A balance sheet

## Results

In discussion, the participants worked towards what came to be called a 'composite' report. The best practice agenda seemed to comprise the items set out in Figure 8.1. It was suggested that achieving 10 out of the 12 might be a very good result, and that to compensate at the margin, institutions with special strengths in any

*Figure 8.2*   ACU 'show and tell'

| | |
|---|---|
| 1. (West Indies) | Community Service Mandate |
| 2. (Southern Africa) | Stakeholder Advisory Group |
| 3. (RSA*) | Student Parliament |
| 4. (Australia) | 70 per cent mature intake |
| 5. (W. Canada) | Community specific research themes |
| 6. (Wales) | Quantitative targets for strategic goals |
| 7. (Australia) | State Partnership Agreement |
| 8. (Australia) | Industry-based learning (IBL), WBL, and 'my attributes' (self-assessment software) |
| 9. (New Zealand) | Senior management accountability |
| 10. (England) | Focus on regional communications |
| 11. (Australia) | Civic engagement in promotion criteria |
| 12. (Australia) | Regional Lobby and Reference Groups |

*Note:* * Republic of South Africa

one or two areas might be allowed to play a 'joker' (scoring double marks).

As a further essay in mutual learning it was decided to identify one highly distinctive feature which each of the participants had bought to the party. Here the aspect of 'cultural embedding' of higher education system shone through most clearly (Figure 8.2 identifies the institutions by country only).

Overall this exercise underlined the 'moving target' quality of considering community and civic engagement on an international basis. The thirst for sound 'benchmarking' frameworks and resulting data was, however, fully evident, and the reporting template served its purpose. Two other such approaches are summarized below (for a helpful introduction to these exercises see Duke 2003).

## Other approaches

In 2002, the University of Minnesota Civic Engagement Task Force reported on an assessment of community–university partnerships, including a useful typology, as set out below.

*Consultative partnerships*
In this type of relationship, a faculty member, unit, department or school has the same relationship to a client as a self-employed or privately established consultant.
*The work the Humphrey Institute does with the legislature and cities and the Extension program on Business, Relationships and Expansion seem to fit into this category of partnerships.*

*Technical Assistance Partnerships*
In this kind of relationship, a client entity has much more comprehensive responsibility for identifying an outcome or product of the relationship.
*The work the University of Minnesota, Crookston is doing with school districts and with natural resource consortia fits into this category of partnerships.*

*Partnership of Convenience*
This is the conceptual converse of the Consultative Partnership in that it is a relationship initiated by an academic entity (faculty member, department, school etc.) with an external party.
*Many community-based research activities – for example, Ken Heyburn's Savvy Caregiver research – fit in this category.*

*Generative Partnership*
This is a relationship between some part of the academy and some external entity that produces something – deliberately vague – that takes on its own life. As such, this third entity may begin to interact independently with each of its progenitors.
*There are a number of striking examples of this kind of partnership. The Community University Health Care Center, the Regional Geriatric Education Centers and the Regional Sustainable Development Partnerships function like this.*

*Partnerships for Mutual Benefit*
In this relationship, an academic and an external entity recognize that each can gain from working on a common project. *The clinical center for interdisciplinary geriatric education is an example of this kind of partnership.*

*Outreach*
In this relationship between academic entities and either organizations (including communities) and/or individuals, the balance of power tilts towards the academic entity.
*Many of the examples provided by the University of Minnesota Extension Service fit this model of partnership.*

*Source:* www.engagement.umn.edu/cope/reports/appendices02.html

To return to the issue as framed by the ACU, the original 'consultation' contains a useful set of 'framing questions' from the then Secretary General (Michael Gibbons) organized in five domains as set out below. Each of these represents an area where the university can test itself, and the environment in which it operates.

*The imperative of engagement*

- mission statement or strategic plan
- formal mechanisms for consultation
- promotion of 'the special value of the academic enterprise'
- links with industry and public services
- academic study of engagement
- evaluation

*Purposes and policies*

- a national forum
- lay/employer role in governance
- funding incentives

- relationship with professional bodies
- regional fora

*The world is our student*

- first-class teaching
- anticipating employment
- feedback from employers
- fostering of 'generic personal and intellectual capabilities'
- national debate on student preparation 'to contribute effectively to the future working world'
- motivation to 'continue learning'
- work-based learning
- professional updating
- funding for 'employability and citizenship'

*The dialogue of theory with practice*

- national research priorities
- influence of 'research-users'
- fostering of community understanding and use of research
- incentives for cooperative research with 'industry, community groups, the professions, government agencies, artists and traders'
- exploitation of 'promising discoveries'
- balanced of central and devolved responsibilities

*Citizens*

- incentives for 'faculty to become engaged with the local community'
- mechanisms for 'open dialogue between university and community leaders'
- roles of students and academics 'such as volunteerism and the arts'
- university projects to respond to community needs
- town and gown' dialogue, including to 'challenge the priorities of the university.'

*Source:* ACU 2001

At the highest level, each of these domains, as well as the Minnesota typology, can be used to evaluate both the national contexts and the 'case studies' in the earlier part of this section. The effect there is to show a subtly different pattern of influences and outcomes in each of the national systems (the UK in Chapter 5, Australia in Chapter 6, and the USA in Chapter 7).

Briefly, the UK has become heavily focused on the search for ear-marked public funding for these sorts of priorities (this is perhaps predictable given overall levels of funding and the tendency for micro-management from outside by funders, as discussed in Chapter 3). Sustainability thus becomes a key preoccupation for institutional management and for the specialists within each team. Locally, in-stitutions are often in fierce competition for national funds. In Australia, the concept of community service is heavily dominated by the fact of regional recruitment (very few students – unlike in the UK – cross state boundaries to study). This gives a powerful sense of local accountability, which is high up the agenda for university leaders. Such leaders have, in recent years, strategically utilized the civic and community agenda to win political support. The system in the USA is, as commentators never tire of reminding us, hugely diverse and strongly stratified: from strongly locally embedded community col-leges, to the nationally recruiting (and highly expensive) elite. However, across this range, institutions have to battle for community support not only when their relatively rich and well-endowed cam-puses are in relatively poor and disadvantaged communities. At the same time curriculum planners can draw on a rich tradition of credit for volunteering, of service-learning and of cooperative course design with employers). Looser patterns of accreditation and a tradition of deferring formal professional education until the second (or post-graduate) cycle help here, as does the tendency for partisan political activity on campus to be encouraged (not least by the politicians themselves).

Other national traditions operate across this range, and indeed extend it. For example: in China the concept of universities 'service to society' is almost entirely predicated on the creation of human capital and the contribution of research to industry; in South Africa higher education struggles under the weight of expectation laid upon it to lead in post-apartheid social transformation; in Bangladesh re-sidential higher education has for long been seen as a variety of national service; in South Korea, there are concerns about the poli-tical power that students could potentially wield, and so on. Special circumstances also apply in those countries where universities refer back to the legal framework (perhaps a single 'higher education law') to govern their activities, as in Finland and Japan. And then there are the waves of 'morphic resonance' (introduced in Chapter 2) that periodically sweep across the global system (of which widening participation – discussed in Chapter 10) is the latest. Perhaps 'Talloires' and its advocates (see the Introduction – Chapter 1) have caught such a wave.

# PART THREE: MANAGING CIVIC AND COMMUNITY ENGAGEMENT

# 9

# MANAGING CIVIC ENGAGEMENT: INSIDE THE ACADEMY

*If the fundamental thesis of this book – that civic and community engagement has re-emerged as part of the inescapable agenda of the modern HEI – is correct, then important questions are raised about its relationship to the internal culture, practice, and priorities of the institutions themselves. This chapter attempts to locate engagement within aspects of the changing 'inner life' of higher education: the inner game of curriculum development; the currently hot question of the student experience; the implications for shared values; and, finally, how the university manages the 'inside-out' elements of its engagement activities.*

## The inner game of higher education

As set out in Chapter 2, universities and colleges are very special institutions in modern society (by modern is meant since the fourteenth century AD). Contrary to some popular beliefs they have always been very practical and responsive places: creating and establishing new knowledge and teaching new skills to cope with changing circumstances. In other words, perhaps more than any other enduring institution in our history, they have proved capable of reinventing themselves to meet new demands. Meanwhile, while each university has its distinctive but changing history, another part of the university enterprise has always remained the same. We have in our business what Einstein called a 'cosmological constant'. There has always been an independent, deeply ethical part of our work that is critical and concerned about enduring values: values such as scientific honesty, openness to new and uncomfortable ideas, tolerance, as well as human emancipation. In other words, if you become a student or a teacher in higher education, you are seriously committed to finding your own way to help to make the world a better place. The ebb and flow between these forces creates a very special kind of 'inner game'.

An introductory word is order on the chosen metaphor (borrowed from Timothy Gallwey's 'inner game of tennis'): the 'inner game' of higher education is the one we choose to play ourselves; not the one we are required to play. It relies on looking at higher education from the 'inside out' rather than the outside in. This is the sphere of action of consenting adults, of self-imposed rules and conventions, of teamwork, and of magnaminity in victory and honour in defeat. It is a deliberate attempt to put on one side – for a moment – the anxieties about funding, about accountability, or about what 'stakeholders' say they want. This chapter starts with a discussion of the resulting 'inner game' of higher education. The objective is to describe some of the forces that construct the identity of the university community itself, and hence the 'third' form of engagement outlined in Chapter 11. It is, of course, a powerful metaphor; following Gallwey there are today 65 items for sale on Amazon with the title 'Inner Game'. 'Winning is overcoming obstacles to reach a goal, but the value in winning is only as great as the goal itself ... So we arrive at the startling conclusion that true competition is identical with true cooperation ... In true competition no person is defeated' (Gallwey 1975: 111).

A similarly powerful metaphor lies in Richard Sennett's discussion of cooperation in ensemble music-making in his wonderful work, *Respect*. There's also no accident that this metaphor is also about 'playing'. Sennett speaks about how musicians learn to respect each other, not because they necessarily like or admire each other, but to achieve a mutual goal, which results from combining their self-respect as craftsmen. Here he is describing the collaboration of the singer Dietrich Fischer-Dieskau and the pianist Gerald Moore in a *lieder* performance:

> Part of what makes both men rare performers is that they have *achieved* mutuality; many musicians have the cooperative impulse, but few manage to translate it into sound. Even more is this true of social life; an enormous gap exists between wanting to act well toward others and doing so ... I argue that in social life as in art, mutuality requires expressive work. It must be enacted, performed.
>
> (Sennett 2003: 59; original emphasis)

Incidentally, in his latest book (*The Culture of the New Capitalism*), Sennett returns to this concept of craftsmanship, as one of his three potential sources of a 'social anchor' in what is otherwise a rather pessimistic view of the prospects for twenty-first-century work and personal identity (the other two are 'narrative' and 'usefulness' – both evocative terms for the arts and humanities). For him 'craftsmanship' is 'doing something well for its own sake'. It is linked with democracy, via the 'citizen-as craftsman', and it is structured around 'commitment'. (It is also interesting that in Britain the origins of non-university tertiary education were very substantially constructed around the notion of 'craft'; in 1850 there were over 600 'Mechanics' Institutes' serving over 100,000 students.)

> It's not simply that the obsessed, competitive craftsman may be committed to doing something well, but more that he or she believes in its objective value. A person can use the words correct or right in describing how well something is done only if he or she believes in an objective standard outside his or her own desires, indeed outside the sphere of rewards from others. Getting something right, even though it may get you nothing, is the spirit of true craftsmanship.
>
> (Sennett 2006: 104, 171, 195)

The opposite of the 'craftsman' in this book is the 'consultant' (and who are those in higher education to disagree?). The latter is a vital tool in what Sennett calls the 'MP3' organization (where the 'laser in the central processing unit is boss'): 'executives at the center of the MP3 machine can shift responsibility for painful decisions away from themselves'. The craftsman 'stands at the opposite pole of the consultant, who sweeps in and out but never nests' (Sennett 2006: 51, 53, 105). There are some lessons here about de-layering and related management approaches in universities, but that is another story.

In exploring the inner game, we need to pull together developments in at least three related areas:

- how graduates and part-time students are seen as actual and potential economic and social actors outside the university (discussed in Chapter 2 from the perspective of different types of 'capital');
- background, capabilities, interests and ambitions of the student body (discussed below); and
- the mode of production in subject and professional areas contributing to undergraduate and postgraduate courses (also discussed below).

The players in the 'inner game' represent three triangular points captured by these domains: students and their interests; staff and in particular their loyalties and commitments to subjects and professional areas; and genuine stakeholders, who have some assets at risk in the overall enterprise.

## The student experience

The 'student experience' is one of those compound concepts that in the UK has begun to take on a life of its own, relatively removed from reality. You can see this in the way it is used by politicians (not least when complaining about 'what students get'), by the funding councils (especially in the context of the National Student Survey – NSS), by institutions (in their prospectuses), and most aggressively by the Higher Education Academy. To quote the latter's strategic plan: 'The Academy's mission is to help institutions, discipline groups and all staff to provide the best possible learning experience for their students.'

The concept is under pressure because it is no longer a singular thing, as it may have been when Michael Oakeshott called it 'the gift of an interval'. It is also one of those things which can sound better than it is (like 'low-start mortgages', 'English middle-order batting', 'gastropub', and 'sun-dried tomatoes'; or in higher education terms, 'the lighter touch' and 'the single conversation').

To begin with a view from outside: as young participation continues to increase (whether or not in the UK we get soon to the 50 per cent target, the affordability of which is increasingly beginning to concern government – as set out in Chapter 3), we in universities need to take a little more account of general sociology of youth.

A good example of the genre is Nick Barham's book, *Disconnected* (Barham 2004). Barham looks at a series of 'interest groups' (drugs, graffiti, joyriding, computer-gaming), which in the words of his subtitle turn 'their backs on everything we thought we knew'. The disturbing thing is that, in a perverse way, these are all learning communities, and very sophisticated at it. Similar things have been said about prisons. What it means is that non-progression after 16 is not, as those who would like to place quotas on General Certificate of Secondary Education (GCSE) and advanced-level (A-level) grades think it is, about innate ability. As a consequence the civic engagement agenda implies that we should be thinking about the 50 per cent of each age cohort who are *not* scheduled to progress to higher education, and thinking hard about why to them what we have to offer is both irrelevant and unattainable (see also the discussion of access and equity in the next chapter).

More generally, the emerging story seems to be that young people in western societies now relate horizontally, or laterally, more than vertically. They relate more effectively to their friends (shades here of E.M. Forster and of Julian Mitchell's 1981 play and 1984 film *Another Country*), to the Internet and to the interactive media in general (including banking services), rather than to 'authority', to their families, and especially to political structures. This does not mean – as dyspeptic right-wing commentators and other dystopians would have it – that they lack moral sense; rather, as John Ahier and his collaborators show brilliantly in their book, *Graduate Citizens?* (Ahier *et al.* 2002), they define 'mutuality' differently. Practically, it has implications for their attitudes and behaviour in terms of consumption, in terms of careers, in terms of conformity, and emphatically in terms of credit. The emphasis here on 'western societies' is deliberate. Elsewhere youth cultures react to these developments in polarized ways, ranging from imitation and envy to rejection, revulsion and revolution.

Returning to the UK, a related 'reality check' concerns mid-career and older students; we need to understand that put together they constitute at least half of the body-count clientele of the system. Comparatively, we have in the UK one of the most diverse student bodies in the world, despite our concerns to the contrary. As Brian Ramsden showed in his contribution to *Higher Education and the Lifecourse*, compared with the countries contributing to *Euro Student 2000*, the UK has:

- the highest proportion of part-time students;
- the oldest average age;
- the highest percentage with declared disabilities;
- the second highest percentage from lower socio-economic backgrounds (after Finland); and
- the second lowest rate of 'local' attendance (including the proportion living in the parental home – also after Finland) (Slowey and Watson 2003: 3–19).

What this also means, in terms of the 'student experience', is that as the system continues to expand, and as traditional 'screening' mechanisms drop away, the higher education population will come to look more like the population at large. There are certain characteristics of this population that we are less well equipped to deal with than others (and than we should be). One is mental health, and a useful initiative tracking this is the Nuffield Foundation's programme on 'time trends in adolescent well-being' (report available on www.nuffieldfoundation.org).

Finally, on this tack, it is important not to fall into the trap of replacing one relatively homogeneous image of the undergraduate population (the Oakeshottian finishing school), with another ('Thatcher's children' or the 'screenage generation'). The extremes have coexisted, and have been catered for by different types of institution for some time. So have all of the points on the spectrum in between. The argument here is for a consultative, and research-based, approach to what students really want and need, and not just a rather patronizing, nostalgic evocation of what commentators (of a certain age) think we most fruitfully received at their stage in life.

Putting these contexts together, several propositions emerge about the nature of the student experience in the UK today.

Proposition one: *students themselves are significantly responsible for the successes of 'mass' higher education, and we should be celebrating their success.* For example, take student and graduate performance – on things like retention (the North American term 'persistence' is a useful one) and on employability (especially the evidence of their growing what were not considered 'graduate jobs' into those which can safely be added to the definition). These very positive outcomes, which politicians and HE leaders record with such pride, are *their* achievement, not just a measure of what institutions do to them.

What those in the institutions *are* responsible for could be called the 'opportunity framework', including some of its structural weaknesses: achievement and continuation at 17; the post-Tomlinson loss of nerve on reform of the 14–19 curriculum; support for adult returners (in, out and 'after' work), and so on (see Watson 2005a). This is where 'supply' and 'demand' overlap, in a quite complex way.

Proposition two: *at their best, and given the chance, students know what they want to do, and their instincts are sound.* This is partly about choice of subjects, where the reports have underlined the difficulties providers have faced (more successfully in recent years) in adjusting to the popularity and unpopularity of certain courses, as set out in Figure 9.1. The 'Media Studies' vogue, in a deeply ironic way, was a *demand*-led phenomenon (it is ironic, because one of the chief charges from the political-industrial complex is that HE does not respond to demand). Meanwhile, inside the institutions, we have difficulty in adapting: the UUK Longer Term Strategy Group *Patterns* reports show how many institutions have chosen to enter a field (like sports science) after the market has peaked (there are now several subject areas where more students are admitted to subjects than applied for them, as revealed by Figure 9.2).

*Figure 9.1*  Percentage full-time first degree students in each subject area, 1994–95 to 2004–05

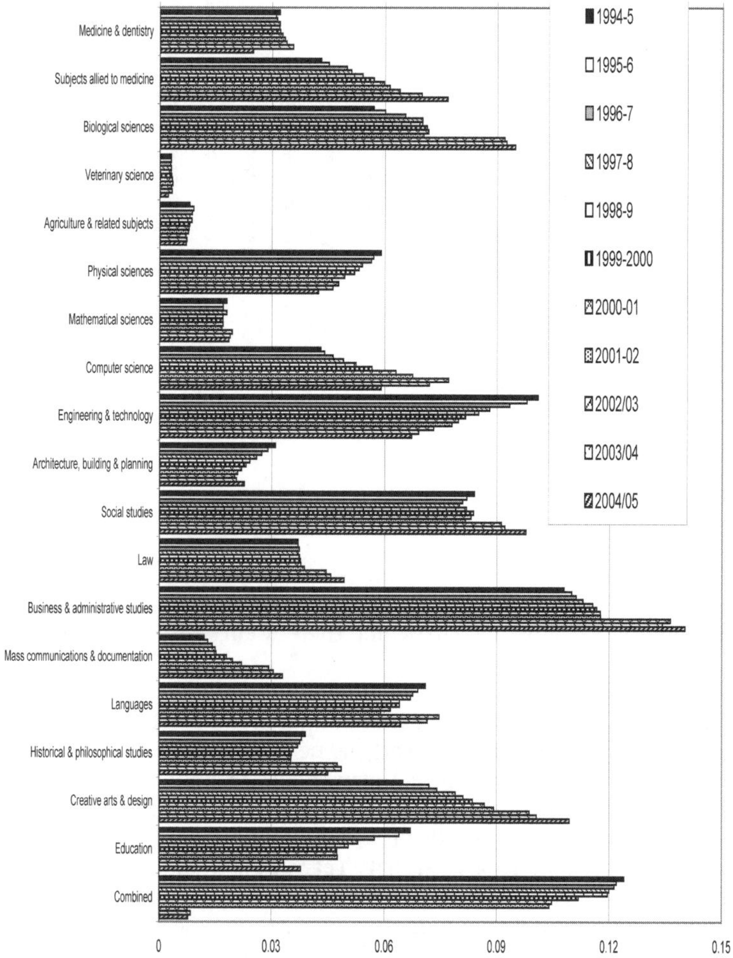

Medicine & dentistry
Subjects allied to medicine
Biological sciences
Veterinary science
Agriculture & related subjects
Physical sciences
Mathematical sciences
Computer science
Engineering & technology
Architecture, building & planning
Social studies
Law
Business & administrative studies
Mass communications & documentation
Languages
Historical & philosophical studies
Creative arts & design
Education
Combined

■ 1994-5
☐ 1995-6
▨ 1996-7
▨ 1997-8
☐ 1998-9
▮ 1999-2000
▨ 2000-01
▨ 2001-02
▨ 2002/03
☐ 2003/04
▨ 2004/05

0      0.03      0.06      0.09      0.12      0.15

*Source:* UUK 2006b: 26

Student choice is also about mode of study, where the sectoral supertanker has to deal with rapid growth in demand for part-time undergraduate and full-time postgraduate courses (see Table 9.1). It is about brands, where, for example, only in relation to public service do foundation degrees (Fd) seem to have high-volume future prospects. The vast majority of current and potential Fd students are full

*Figure 9.2* Ratio of UK domiciled applicants to acceptances through UCAS, 1995 and 2004 entry

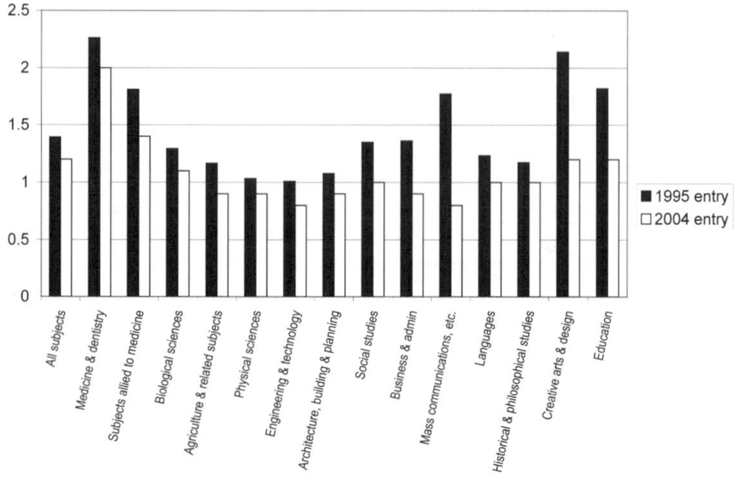

*Source:* UUK 2006b: 57

time and in the public sector; while the much touted private-sector trailblazers have small enrolments, only short-term prospects, and flirt with being 'closed' courses (and thereby currently unfundable by the HEFCE).

Finally, it is about choice of institutions. 'Hard to reach' groups remain concentrated in one particular part of the sector (as revealed in Figure 9.3). Why is it that nearly 60 per cent of the ethnic minority students in the whole of the country choose to study in London and the South East (Watson 2006)? To quote the Teaching and Learning Research Programme (TLRP) project, SOMUL (the Social and Organizational Mediation of University Learning): what are the implications for the access agenda as it is currently conceptualized of the hypothesis (securely founded in American research) that 'the amount of learning is not related to "quality" rankings of institutions (you won't necessarily learn more if you go to a posh place)'? This, for example, is how John Brennan, the project leader describes two sociology students contributing to the project:

- An old university with a good reputation, a nice campus and a high entry requirement. A school leaver: pleased to be there, with a lifetime of educational success, relaxed about the degree, excited to be away from home and not really interested in Sociology – therefore, integration with university model [that is, identifying more with the university than with the subject]. S/he's not sure that Sociology is the best option and wishes it had been less 'woolly' more vocational, but at least s/he chose the right university.

- A new university with a lot of economic deprivation; mostly local students living at home, mature, entering via access routes, HNDs etc; if A-levels, not good grades. A mature student who said how fascinated she was by how sociology impacted on everything in her life – the things she said and did – and how it had opened her eyes to what other people were saying/meaning/doing. Not involved in university life,

*Table 9.1*   Overall change by mode and level, 1994-95 to 2003–04

|  | UK | England | Wales | Scotland | Northern Ireland |
|---|---|---|---|---|---|
| % change in number of PGs,* 1994–95 to 2003–04 | 56.2 | 58.2 | 62.3 | 44.0 | 30.4 |
| % change in number of UGs,** 1994–95 to 2003–04 | 39.9 | 39.5 | 49.2 | 35.9 | 50.0 |
| % change in all students, 1994–95 to 2003–04 | 43.4 | 43.5 | 51.6 | 37.8 | 45.2 |
| *Change in part-time numbers* | | | | | |
| % change in numbers of part-time PGs, 1994–95 to 2003–04 | 47.6 | 47.4 | 79.0 | 45.2 | 22.4 |
| % change in numbers of part-time UGs, 1994–95 to 2003–04 | 104.1 | 93.8 | 235.1 | 200.7 | 162.9 |
| *Change in full-time numbers* | | | | | |
| % change in numbers of full-time PGs, 1994–95 to 2003–04 | 69.9 | 75.8 | 43.5 | 42.4 | 48.6 |
| % change in numbers of full-time UGs, 1994–95 to 2003–04 | 20.6 | 21.0 | 13.3 | 19.2 | 30.1 |

*Notes:*
* Postgraduates.
** Undergraduates.

*Source:* UUK 2006b: 16

not necessarily confident she'll pass as had not had a lifetime of educational success – therefore stronger on academic engagement.

(UUK 2006a: 20; for details on SOMUL see www.open.ac.uk/cheri/SOMULhome.htm)

*Figure 9.3*   Percentage of young full-time first degree entrants from NS-SEC* Classes 4, 5, 6 and 7, 2003–04

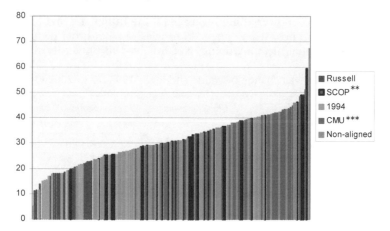

*Source:* UUK 2005: 55

Notes:
 * National Statistics – socio-economic classification
 ** Standing Committee of Principals (now Guild HE)
 *** Campaign for Mainstream Universities

So we should pay careful heed when students do not want to do what their elders and betters think they should; we should learn from the reasons why; and we should offer them a greater degree of trust.

Another trap is the older generation's attempt to impose the portfolio career on a generation whose trajectory towards a stable single occupation or employer may be slightly longer or more complex, but in fact has the same destination (see the latest report of the Tomorrow Group, *Working in the Twenty-First Century* – Tomorrow Group 2005: 93–100). One of the most painful experiences for university leaders is to sit in on sessions during which old men in suits, who themselves have had anything but a portfolio career, have told younger people (usually not in suits) that this is the best they can expect. Empirically, they are wrong, and they should not be allowed to get away with it.

There is also an interesting issue here about student in-strumentalism. Today's undergraduates do know that the world does not owe them a living (as perhaps it did when no more than 10–12 per cent of each age cohort became graduates). Simply having a degree will not be enough. But that does not mean that their view of 'vocation-alism' will be the same as that of the older generation (the Engineering institutions in particular have been slow to understand this).

This leads on to proposition three: *we need to be particularly careful about 'skills', on the way into and on the way out of university.* There is plenty of nostalgic and ideologically loaded analysis of what new and graduating students cannot do; there is precious little account taken of what today's screenagers *can* do; that many of their predecessors and at least some of their teachers cannot. Most of this has to do with ICT and with what the latter would (wrongly) dismiss as 'toys'. It will not be long before we are no longer talking about ICT as if it is something 'over there'. It will be an integral and embedded aspect of all subjects.

Jason Frand's seminal essay on the 'information age mind-set' is one of the most arresting accounts of this dilemma (Frand 2000). Frand's conceit is based on the definition by Alan Kay of technology as 'anything that wasn't around when you were born' (compare your own experience of the telephone, and of the personal computer). All of his 'ten attributes reflecting values and behaviours' will be familiar to parents of early twenty-first-century screenagers (particularly re-sonant is 'Nintendo not logic' – you learn at a computer game by endlessly failing). Sadly the same cannot be said of many of their teachers. The Engineering Professors Conference complains every year about the calculus that first-year students could do 20 years ago but cannot now. They never look at the reciprocal. Just what skills do this new generation (whose identity is significantly recorded on *My Space* in the UK or *Face Book* in the USA) bring with them that their predecessors did not, and how relevant are they? How revealing is the invention of a mobile phone ring tone (the mosquito tone – winner of a Ig Nobrl award in 2006) that cannot be heard by most people over the age of 20 (Menand 2006)? Figure 9.4 incorporates the full list.

Proposition four: *credentialism counts, and students know it.* Look at the growth in early re-registration for postgraduate and post-experience courses in Table 9.1 (what HEFCE Chief Executive Howard Newby once called 'the privatized fourth year'). There is another lesson from the Tomorrow Group here. In the knowledge economy, you need an increasing level of qualification to stay in the same place. From the point of view of the knowledge economy, this is not necessarily a bad thing.

*Figure 9.4*   The 'information age mindset'

- Computers are not technology
- Internet better than television
- Reality no longer real
- Doing rather than knowing
- Nintendo over logic
- Multi-tasking way of life
- Typing rather than handwriting
- Staying connected
- Zero tolerance for delays
- Consumer/creator blurring

*Source:* Based on Frand 2000

Proposition five: *students now invariably work for money, and not just in response to changes in fees and student support.* They want to sustain lifestyles. This process, incidentally, starts in sixth forms (where about three-quarters of students now have jobs) and perhaps even earlier. What is more the effects appear finally to be settling down. Data from the University of Brighton (Table 9.2) show that excessive hours have tailed off with a majority of working students settling on about 15 hours a week (compared with the 12 which the university recommends – and which the House of Commons Select Committee later endorsed).

We should certainly be tracking all the current studies about student debt, but also those about debt and debt propensity in the wider society (where we do not see debt aversion, rather debt joy). We should be similarly careful about the more recent HE moral panic – the isolated occurrence of 'studentification' of residential communities (discussed in Chapter 11). There's a wider context here too, seen in the 2001 census trend towards single occupancy.

Proposition six: *students care.* As suggested above, they are only rarely 'Thatcher's children', or the North American variant, 'the Organization Kid'. What has confused a lot of people is that they could not care less about organized party politics. Some smarter students' unions have spotted this. What does get them going is concern about the environment, and their obligations to their friends.

Students are also ahead of many institutional managers in international perspectives. How much have we thought about those campuses which now serve students (and there are many of them – see Table 4.2) from over 100 different countries?

So what has to change – and what should stay the same in terms of our responsibility for the 'student experience'?

For example, in terms of the 'whole student experience', where

*Table 9.2* University of Brighton – student finance surveys (percentages)

| | 2nd year students with debts of over £1000 (2004 prices) | Uptake of student loans | Regular employment in term time | Use of a car | Use of a computer | Mobile phone ownership |
|---|---|---|---|---|---|---|
| 2005 | 50 | 86 | 61<br>16+ hours per week-32 | 53 | 91 | 94 |
| 2004 | 54 | 87 | 53<br>16+ hours per week-25.1 | 49 | 90 | 98 |
| 2003 | 45 | 88 | 52<br>16+ hours per week-28 | 48 | 93 | 96 |
| 2002 | 47 | 89 | 54<br>16+ hours per week-29 | 46 | 80 | 93 |
| 2000 | 41 | 78 | 51<br>16+ hours per week-32 | 52 | 74 | |
| 1998 | 42 | 68 | 45<br>16+ hours per week-31 | 47 | 66 | |
| 1996 | 30 | 56 | 36<br>16+ hours per week-20 | | | |
| 1994 | 22 | 43 | 34<br>16+ hours per week-18 | | | |
| 1992 | 17 | 40 | 30<br>16+ hours per week-11 | | | |

*Source:* Pemberton and Winn 2005

does this leave the panoply of institutional 'student services'? Just as they have emerged from late twentieth-century Cinderella status, are they about to be thrust back again, as a consequence of more brittle, ligitation-averse, concepts of customer care? The points made earlier about mental health are relevant here. A huge temptation is to fall into the trap (dug for us originally by Lee Harvey at Sheffield Hallam University) of regarding student 'satisfaction' as a proxy for quality (Harvey 1999). (It may be too late: on the basis that what Australia does today, New Labour will try to do before sunset, look at the role played by student satisfaction data within their DEST Teaching and Learning Performance Fund – www.dest.gov.au/sectors/higher_ education/policy_issues_reviews/key_issues/learning_teaching/ltpf/.)

It is also salutary to learn what students want their additional fee income spent on (see Figure 9.5): the top items are books, IT and security (according to the 2005 UNITE survey); certainly not higher salaries for staff.

Meanwhile, nothing said here is intended to undermine the traditional essence of higher education (what is genuinely 'higher' about it) in terms of the evolving 'conversation' between more and less experienced learners. Indeed, the higher education enterprise could be said to be a model of the form of conversation, the loss of which is lamented by Stephen Miller in his elegiac *Conversation: A History of a Declining Art* (Miller 2006). Miller draws extensively on another theme of Michael Oakeshott's: for him conversation is 'an unrehearsed intellectual adventure'; as with gambling 'its significance lies neither in winning or losing, but in wagering' (quoted in Baker 2006: 4). 'Conversation' also lies at the heart of the challenge of cosmopolitanism raised in Chapter 4. As Kwame Anthony Appiah concludes in his *Cosmopolitanism*, 'conversation' is vital to value adjudication, especially in circumstances where 'there are some values that are, and should be universal, just as there are lots of values that are, and must be local' (Appiah 2006: xxi). In these statements Oakeshott and Appiah come very close to capturing the essence of higher-level learning and teaching.

We do, however, have to think hard about some developments that might be damaging in this context, such as the drive for secure and frequent summative assessment and its effects on the learning that can come from more generous and sensitive formative assessment. We need to cling on to notions like joy, fun, and even mercy, alongside 'accountability' and the relentless march of uniform 'good practice'.

In this connection, it is crucial not to ignore the 'staff experience'. Mentioned above is a possible dislocation between the staff and the student experience. One (highly positive) outcome of significant expansion over the last 20 years is that such dissonance will reduce. The average age of teaching staff in the UK is dropping; it is now 42.7 (see HESA 2004/05: table 23a). Let us assume that it is 40 by 2015. At that stage, most of the teaching force will have been born in 1975, gone to university in 1993 and graduated in 1996 or 1997. Mass, or universal, higher education will hold little fear for them, to say nothing of the

*Figure 9.5*   The views of students about what additional funding from differential tuition fees should be spent on

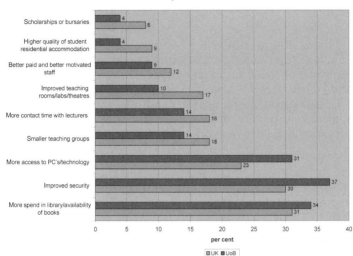

*Source:* Based on UNITE 2005
Note: UoB = University of Brighton

personal computer. Evidence also suggests (not least because of the emergence of 'new', applied subjects) that they will more regularly have experience outside higher education as well as within it.

How does this affect what we try to teach and how we try to teach it? In the case of subjects and disciplines, perhaps the most influential conceptual advance of the last decade is Michael Gibbons and collaborators' notion of 'mode 2' knowledge production, summarized in Table 9.3.

*Table 9.3*   Mode 1 and mode 2

| Mode 1 | Mode 2 |
|---|---|
| Pure | Applied |
| Disciplinary | Problem-centred |
| Homogeneous | Transdisciplinary |
| Expert-led | Heterogeneous |
| Supply-driven | Hybrid |
| Hierarchical | Demand-driven |
| Peer-reviewed | Entrepreneurial |
| University-based | Network-embedded |

*Source:* Gibbons *et al.* 1994

Among other things, this set of developments is going to make the traditional discussions about the separation of teaching and research anachronistic. We will have mode 2 teaching, along with mode 2 knowledge production. To quote SOMUL again:

> rapidly shifting patterns of disciplinary knowledge and changing principles of course organisation appear to be creating complex and often looser curricular offerings within institutions. Boundaries exist (i.e. constraints and rules about what can be studied) but they are no longer clear-cut and coterminous with previous disciplinary and organisational structures.
>
> (SOMUL 2005: 6)

In several of these respects, it is arguable that the arts and humanities have already arrived. The research and teaching *agenda* for these perennially popular subjects are inextricably intertwined. As Cary Nelson and Stephen Watt declare in their *Academic Keywords: A Devil's Dictionary for Higher Education*, 'research and writing together *produce* the contemporary intelligibility of the humanities' (Nelson and Watt 1999: 221; original emphasis).

What will this re-engineering entail? To return to the triangle I invoked at the beginning of this section, it will have to include thinking hard about students (what they want, as well as what we think they need), about staff (and their professional as well as disciplinary loyalties), about natural (and other) alliances, and any other opportunities and threats.

To return to the beginning, there is an optimistic tone to this evocation of the inner game. For more dystopian commentators, today's game is either a replacement of one ritual by another (for such type I pessimism see Mary Evans or Robert Stevens), or more seriously the loss of a more serious, complex and rewarding game (Evans 2004; Stevens 2004). The classic type II witness is Allan Bloom, in his *The Closing of the American Mind* (1998).

> Students these days are, in general, nice. I choose the word carefully. They are not particularly moral or noble. Such niceness is a facet of democratic character when times are good. Neither war nor tyranny nor want has hardened them or made demands upon them. The wounds and rivalries caused by class distinction have disappeared along with any strong sense of class ... Students these days are pleasant, friendly and if not great-souled, at least not particularly mean-spirited. Their

primary preoccupation is themselves, understood in the narrowest sense.

(Bloom 1998: 82–3)

This is quoted approvingly by Dennis Hayes (another type-II dystopian) in his contribution to Arthur with Bohlin (2005: 117–34). I do not think either type of dystopianism is empirically correct in the UK case, but such a counter-argument has to be made responsibly and carefully. The case for the defence relies crucially on trusting the experience and the ambitions of students, including in terms of the kind of engagement which they find relevant and exciting.

In April 2006 the members of the Council of University Deans of Arts and Humanities (CUDAH – now CUDASSH, the Council of University Deans of Arts, Social Sciences and Humanities) came together to attempt just such a counter-argument, by debating the state of the 'inner game'. Their intention was to identify both positive lines of development (to be encouraged and further developed) and negative lines (and how to contain and overcome them). In the course of the discussion they articulated some new rules for the game, including the following:

- improve the clarity of both the formal and informal 'learning contract';
- identify both 'core' (essential) and 'peripheral' aspects of the curriculum, and as a result the practical 'limits of negotiation';
- focus relentlessly on the quality of learning support (not just libraries and IT, but also elements like academic counselling, surgeries and 'drop-in' opportunities, and the like);
- rebalance the relationship between formative and summative assessment (strongly towards the former);
- be less prescriptive about the speed and sequence of curricular experience;
- never forget the principles of the 'conversation'; and above all
- remember the core values of the exercise.

It is this final injunction that leads into the next section.

## The question of values

Aware as we are of the values of the inner game, how far should we codify and declare them to the community outside. On what can the community rely, in moral and ethical terms?

In 1968 the late Lord Eric Ashby was Master of Clare College,

Cambridge, and Vice-Chancellor of the university. (For a scholarly account of Ashby's immense contribution to the wider HE world see Silver 2003: 151–73; for his still highly relevant analysis of the academic estate see Ashby 1959: *passim*). At the Association of Commonwealth Universities in Sydney that year he delivered an address, part of which was later printed in the journal *Minerva*, under the title 'A Hippocratic oath for the academic profession' (Ashby 1969). Nearly 40 years later it has a contemporary resonance as we struggle with the question of whether or not society's legitimate expectations of higher education should be codified.

So what are these commitments, in philosophical, more particularly ethical terms? Is it possible to distil the essence of higher education institutions' values and ethical commitments? Is there an 'academic oath' functionally equivalent to the doctor's Hippocratic oath? Ashby thought that there was. He thought that it lay in the higher education 'teacher's duty to his pupils' to inculcate 'the discipline of constructive dissent'. 'It has to be a constructive dissent which fulfils an overriding condition: it must shift the state of opinion about the subject in such a way that the experts are prepared to concur.' This led him to a firm defence of academic freedom: 'Innovative thinking is unpopular and dangerous. So society has to be indulgent to its universities; it must permit some professors to say silly and unimportant things so that a few professors can say wise and important things' (Ashby 1969: 64). Ashby's focus was on the teacher. Some institutions in the USA believe that such an oath is even more about students, to the extent of requiring graduates to affirm certain propositions about how they will proceed to live their lives in the light of their 'academic' experience.

Another approach is more relativistic. It will stress context, the potential effects of *force majeure* (consider the German universities' response to Nazi edicts), or the need to respond to what 'funders', 'customers' or 'stakeholders' think and say they want. Institutions will claim to have sticking-points, but they will also be willing to negotiate and to compromise. This approach to ethics will – at its best – be one of 'progressive engagement' rather than (literally) dogmatic assessment and response. There is a powerful sense of such a tendency in the Institute of Business Ethics (IBE) and Council for Industry and Higher Education (CIHE) document, *Ethics Matters* (IBE/CIHE 2005). (Incidentally, a pedant could have fun with the title: is it that 'ethics matter' – in which case we should decide what to do about them – or a report on the 'matter of ethics' – in which case we might be less certain about our approach?) The Report states categorically: 'Universities and colleges are complex and autonomous organisations, each with a distinct history and culture. Ethical issues and priorities will not be the same in all institutions and each HEI will need to tackle ethical concerns in a way that makes sense for its own organisation' (IBE/CIHE 2005: 7). To say this is, of course, to commit to a certain philosophical view of ethics: that they will be situational, and to an extent provisional. It is a view that resonates well with certain characteristics of the university project and community: that it is always wrestling with complex and often 'wicked' issues. It is not, however, the only view. Others would argue that ethical issues and priorities *are* the same in all institutions, painful and awkward though this might be for their managers and many of their members; that the question of 'managing ethical issues' does not arise: there is simply the issue of managing their *consequences*. If this dialogue is to be worthy of the name, it needs to accept that keeping ethical commitments will be hard, and may have negative effects on the bottom line. Zygmunt Bauman has, for example, proposed a set of 'invariant values', as follows:

- autonomy;
- critical reflection;
- dialogue;
- disinterestedness;
- mutuality;
- collegiality;
- community;
- equality;
- a shared concern for the common good; and
- a commitment to the ongoing, long-term learning relationship (Robinson and Katalushi 2005: 263).

This is to set the bar appropriately high. Most importantly, institutional leaders should not sink into the pre-emptive, damage-limitation mindset that has come to characterize reactions to some legal and related codes. That way may lie the surface compliance traps of speech codes and political correctness, as well as the displacement effect of hiding behind other people's responsibilities (in his recent book, Bruce Macfarlane reports on how many academics are relieved when the responsibility for ethical judgement is taken away from them, and dealt with formally at a different level in the organization – Macfarlane 2005: 118). At the same time, as the Chair of the European University Association/American Council of Education (EUA/ACE) conference on 'charting the course between public service and commercialisation: prices, values and quality' reminded delegates: 'as we preserve our values, we should remind ourselves that they are those of a university, not a seminary' (EUA/ACE 2004: 39).

So there are problems with both of these approaches: the Benthamite calculus and the Kantian counsel of perfection. Yet another approach (it would perhaps be too much to call it the 'third way') has been set out by Bruce Macfarlane. Following Alasdair MacIntyre, he sets out a list of 'virtues' in *Teaching with Integrity: The Ethics of Higher Education Practice* (Macfarlane 2005: 128–9). Each has a virtuous 'mean', as well as potential defects of 'vice' and 'excess':

- respectfulness;
- sensitivity;
- pride;
- courage;
- fairness;
- openness;
- restraint; and
- collegiality.

The problem here for many will be that it turns being an academic into a form of moral rearmament. Macfarlane's goal is 'the development of the moral character of lecturers in higher education' (2005: 145). Many will be uncomfortable about an approach which stresses 'what people should *be* rather than what they ought to *do*' (Macfarlane 2005: 35).

As a contribution to the debate, there follows an attempt to scope out what the ten commandments (Figure 9.6) given (by whom?) to a higher education institution might be. The intention is in no sense satirical, or even sceptical. In technical terms, this is to take a *deontological* view of ethics (concerned with obligation) rather than an *axiological* (concerned with judgements of value). As discussed in Chapter 11, universities and colleges can choose to behave well, or badly, and it is in our social as well as moral interests to help them to do the former.

*Figure 9.6* The higher education 'commandments'

- *Strive to tell the truth.*
- *Take care in establishing the truth.*
- *Be fair.*
- *Always be ready to explain.*
- *Do no harm.*
- *Keep your promises.*
- *Respect your colleagues, your students, and especially your opponents.*
- *Sustain the community.*
- *Guard your treasure.*
- *Never be satisfied.*

At this stage, a joke about Moses' first words after coming down the mountain may be in order: 'The good news is that I kept him down to ten; the bad news is that adultery is still in.' The academic equivalent is that we 'kept her down to ten, but accountability is still in'.

*Strive to tell the truth.* 'Academic freedom', in the sense of following difficult ideas wherever they may lead, is possibly the fundamental 'academic' value.

*Take care in establishing the truth.* Adherence to scientific method is critical here (as in the use of evidence, and 'falsifiability' principle), but so too is the concept of social scientific 'warrant', and the search for 'authenticity' in the humanities and arts (leading, in particular, to concerns about when rhetoric and persuasion take over independently and in advance of the secure establishment of the grounds for conviction).

*Be fair.* This is about equality of opportunity, non-discrimination, and perhaps even affirmative action. Along with 'freedom' in the academic value-system goes 'respect for persons'.

*Always be ready to explain.* Academic freedom is a 'first amendment' and not a 'fifth amendment' right; it is about freedom of speech and not about protection from self-incrimination (Watson 2000: 85–7). It does not absolve any member of the academic community from the obligation to explain his or her actions, and as far as possible their consequences. Accountability is inescapable, and should not be unreasonably resisted.

*Do no harm.* This is where the assessment of consequences cashes out (and presents our nearest equivalent to the Hippocratic oath, to strive 'not to harm but to help'). It is about non-exploitation, either of human subjects, or of the environment. It underpins other notions like 'progressive engagement'. It helps with really wicked issues like the use of animals in medical experiments.

*Keep your promises.* As suggested above, 'business' excuses for retreating from or unreasonably seeking to renegotiate agreements are much less acceptable in an academic context.

*Respect your colleagues, your students, and especially your opponents.* Working in an academic community means listening as well as speaking, seeking always to understand the other point of view, and ensuring that rational discourse is not derailed by prejudice, by egotism, or by bullying of any kind.

*Sustain the community.* All the values so far expressed are deeply communal. Obligations that arise are not just to the subject or professional community, or even to the institution in which you might be working at any one time, but to the family of institutions that make up the university sector, nationally and internationally.

*Guard your treasure.* University and college communities, and those responsible for leading and managing them, are in the traditional sense 'stewards' of real and virtual assets, and of the capacity to continue to operate responsibly and effectively.

*Never be satisfied.* Academic communities understood the principles of 'continuous improvement' long before it was adopted by 'management' literature. They also understand its merciless and asymptotic nature. The academic project will never be complete or perfect.

In other words, the claim is that there exist value domains which are special to higher education, and which in wider contexts constitute higher education's contributions to civil society in all of its endeavours.

One domain is clearly about how knowledge is effectively and responsibly created, tested and used. Another is about how people responsibly interact with each other (including what they take from the university when they move outside it). And a third is about the institutional presence of universities and colleges in a wider society (as discussed in Chapters 10 and 11), in other words about their civic and community engagement activities.

An important consideration is how far these injunctions are culturally specific. Are they inescapably 'nested' in a western, perhaps even an Anglo-Saxon, view of the context and of the possibilities of a university culture? After much reflection (and some useful advice), I think not; except in one vital respect. They will not work where the institution's primary purpose is dogmatic instruction, not least from a doctrinal point of view. At least since the European Enlightenment, systematic reference to (and validation by) revealed religion will undermine both the universally agreed mode of inquiry (of knowledge creation, testing and use) and the intended destination (which for this value system needs always to be provisional).

Absent these constraining conditions, the commandments seem to work. They also link with aspects of the inner game. These include the core role of the conversation and the principle of mutual respect (between staff and student members of the university; between institutions; between national systems; and between universities and their communities).

## Managing civic engagement: 'inside-out' perspectives

Based upon the case studies in Part Two there is a long list of civic 'service' possibilities with which universities and colleges can engage.

Some of these will be simply about perceived *civic duty*, as when students and staff work as volunteers. Often the specific areas in which they do volunteer will draw upon the intellectual capital of the institution, as when students tutor school pupils or run homework clubs in areas connected with their studies, or when staff members take on governance responsibilities in sectors where they have direct expertise.

Others will be directly embedded in the *curriculum*, as when credit can be earned for structured volunteering, or more programmatically when work-based learning has a civic or community application. The American model of service-learning represents the fullest development of this theme. Community-based projects and dissertations can also be negotiated.

More broadly the institution's programme of *research, development and business support* can be strategically orientated to serve civic and community needs.

Across all three of these core domains (personal civic duty, curriculum development, and research, development and 'third-leg' activity) there is likely to be a special set of relationships which develop with other parts of the public sector: schools; further education; medicine and health; police and probation services; and youth and community. In many local authority areas this will intimately tie higher education into the development of integrated children's services.

Meanwhile there is the important dimension of *shared and open access facilities*, in areas like sport, the arts, libraries and information technology.

Finally the university or college has a direct influence upon both the *physical and business* environment.

All these domains need to be actively fostered and managed, as it were from the 'inside out'.

It is a sad truth that, in common with almost all public services (and those parts of the charitable and voluntary sector which depend upon public funds for even the smallest part of their activity), the only things that can be valued are those which can be measured. As a result, the search for secure, comparable metrics for positive university–community interaction has become a little like the search for the Holy Grail.

The 'activities' which can be measured include volunteering, service learning, community-related research and development and consultancy, provision of facilities, cultural programmes, and so on. If metrics are required, the sector can certainly deliver them. A good example is sport, where a recent survey showed in one year nearly 30 million individual visits by members of the public to HEI sports facilities, and the availability of those facilities (which, of course, simultaneously sustain education, training and research) to the public for about 70 per cent of the times during which they are open (Universities UK 2004a). Some universities have carried such joint ventures even further, as with Leeds Metropolitan's sponsorship of the new refurbished Headingley Stadium, echoing their pioneering role in physical education in the new title of 'Headingley Carnegie' (Wilson, A. 2006), or the University of Phoenix's purchase of the naming rights to the Stadium of the Arizona Cardinals (Blumenstyk 2006). What measures of this kind will rarely do, however, is to supply the kind of fine-grained differentiation between individual institutional performance that equates to the RAE.

This is how an HEFCE working party 'to derive Third Stream social, civic and cultural indicators' described the desiderata in June 2004. The prerequisites for such an allocation process include:

- a representative basket of indicators which recognise the diversity of the HE sector;
- sufficient robustness in the indicators to give confidence as informers of funding decisions;
- ease of application, both in the gathering of the data and interpreting it;
- a very close fit between what the indicators identify and what the economy and society needs from the HE sector's third stream of activity (HEFCE 2004).

There are some candidates out there to meet these requirements, but they all seem to have flaws: for example, by measuring activity rather than impact; by being susceptible to data manipulation or capture by idiosyncratic institutional interest; or even by reverting to 'compensatory' entitlement (we do not do much research or direct business service, so we must be good at supporting the community). They also fall down when institutions – as the best of them do – strategically cooperate to serve a particular community. The high priestess of the 'measuring community contributions' movement is Marilyn Wedgwood of Manchester Metropolitan University (Wedgwood 2003, 2006).

Wedgwood's approach is basically to offer descriptive models of activity domains. This has a valuable taxonomic function, as set out

*Figure 9.7*   Wedgwood's third stream taxonomy

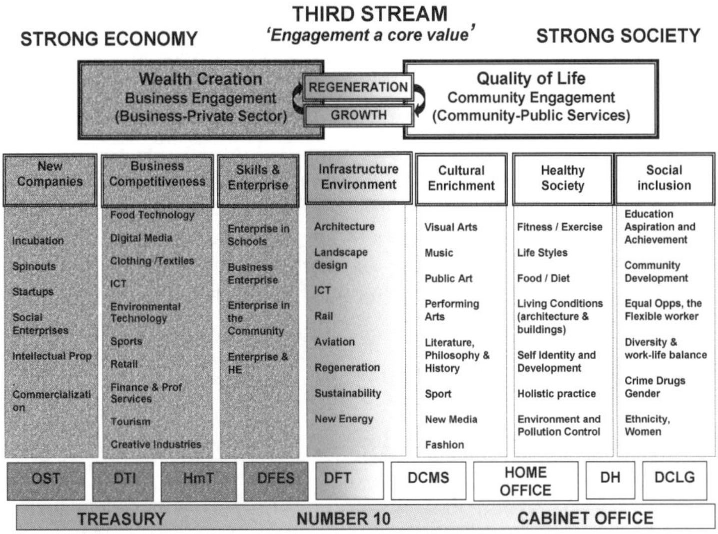

*Source:* Wedgwood 2006: 139

*Figure 9.8*   A Wedgwood activity map

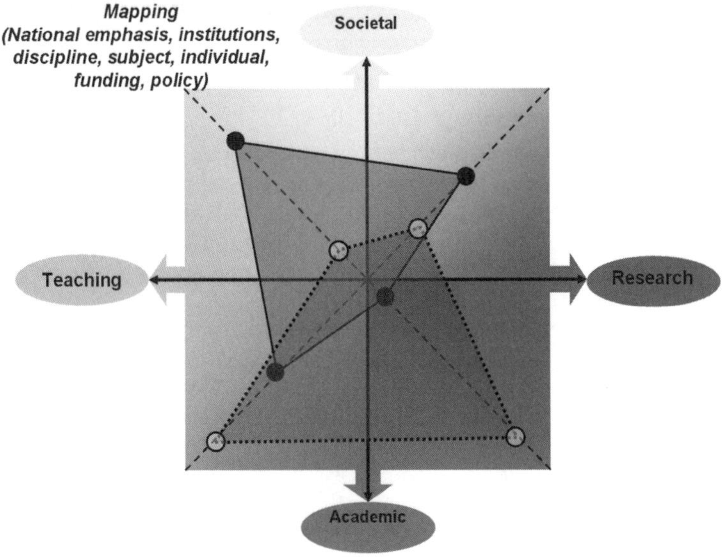

*Source:* Wedgwood 2006: 145

in Figure 9.7. Wedgwood's scheme also allows institutions to 'plot' their activity, as set out in Figure 9.8.

As an exercise, approaches like this are emphatically in their early days; we have yet to get to decent worked examples of the models, which will hold their own against the big beasts of the third stream: business and industry interaction. However, there is some movement.

The University of Cambridge has made an honourable start, with its *Community Engagement Report 2003–4*. This has made public an internal survey, designed in association with members of the Russell Group (although, at the time of writing, Cambridge is the only member not only to report internally, but also to publicize its record) (Wilson, P. 2006). Figure 9.9 sets out some of the headline results from a survey, which approached 147 'units' (departments, colleges, and student societies) of which 93 (63 per cent) responded.

*Figure 9.9* University of Cambridge Community Engagement, 2003–04

---

- Monetary value of 'community engagement': £2,992,841
- Number of beneficiary individuals: 464,465
- Total charitable donations: £65,619
- Total raised by fund-raising activities: £183,980
- Number of staff serving as trustees or governors: 40
- Number of student volunteers involved in 'social inclusion': 962

---

*Source:* University of Cambridge 2004

This is self-consciously a first shot at a difficult exercise, and it is important to allow for this. However, it is also important to recognize (and seek to overcome) some weaknesses. First, this is a voluntary, unaudited survey rather than an account behind which the university can stand definitively. Secondly, there are obvious tensions around what it is appropriate (and possible) to include. For example, distribution of the HEFCE Active Community Fund (which comes into the institution on a formulaic basis) is included, as is all course-work reported on which involves work placements. Meanwhile, there are understandable concerns about whether the university's international ('world-class') mission is possible to incorporate; it is no accident that 41 per cent of the activity recorded is related to public education and another 36 per cent to the community and charitable sector. Thirdly, there is the classic 'self-study' dilemma of knowing not only how well the institution *is* doing against chosen criteria, but also how well it *could* be doing. We are told that the 'degree of commitment by students to community activities ... is astonishing' – but how do we know (University of Cambridge 2004: 21)? Some of the numbers in Figure 9.9 look big; others (like the estimated proportion of staff involved) frankly look small. Above all, it is hard to shake the feeling that at this stage the exercise is more about self-promotion than critical self-study. There are for example no targets set, and no analysis of gaps or weaknesses. The stated objectives include to:

- communicate the university's work to the public;
- maintain good relations with the communities in which we live and work;
- provide learning and personal development and enrichment opportunities for students and staff;
- help maintain a competitive advantage over other universities;
- lead to new opportunities for learning and research;
- challenge negative perceptions about Cambridge being elite;
- strengthen the local economy and increase social cohesion, with the practical benefits that brings to the university; and
- lead to better recruitment, retention and diversification of students and staff (University of Cambridge 2004: 25).

It would be interesting to know the order of priority which the Cambridge community itself would put on these objectives.

The University of Hertfordshire has taken a different approach, working with its local authority (Welwyn Hatfield Council) to produce a study of the *Economic and Social Impact of the University of Hertfordshire on Welwyn Hatfield* (PACEC 2004). The important feature here is a willingness to look at weaknesses, and how to overcome them, as well as strengths to be celebrated. The objectives are to explore 'the short run impact on jobs supported by the University; the social impact of the University on the local and wider community, and (importantly) the long term impacts derived from developing relationships with industry and public sector organisations' (PACEC 2004: 6). There is also a mature sensitivity to the potential gap between perception and reality: the report 'highlights instances when it can be shown that objective facts are consistent or at odds with perceptions' (PACEC 2004: 7).

Some of the hits are obvious, and related to the classic multiplier effect. The calculation is that the university creates an additional 3800 'knock-on' jobs to add to its 2200 direct employees. Student volunteering puts the equivalent of 500 full-time volunteers into the community. The creation of a university bus service – initially to take the pressure off commuting staff and students – has become a key public service (carrying 66 per cent of passengers not connected with the university). Meanwhile there is recognition, contrary to some popular expectations, that the university is not disproportionately responsible for crime and anti-social behaviour, and that casual student employment is not significantly responsible for 'displacing' opportunities for community members (PACEC 2004: 10, 15, 29, 31, 35).

The relative misses are faced head on: the effect of 'buy to rent to students'; heavy commuting pressure in term time; on-street parking problems; and tensions over cultural diversity. On the latter point, 25 per cent of Hatfield residents view the increase in the ethnic minority population as a result of the university as 'negative', and 20 per cent as 'positive'. When and how can they discuss this (PACEC

*Figure 9.10* The University of Hertfordshire Impact Grid

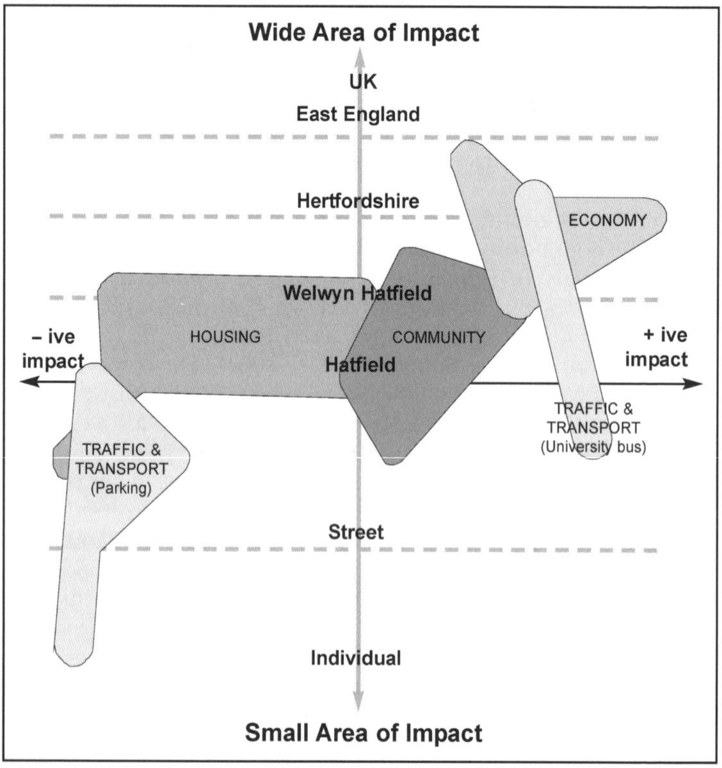

*Source:* PACEC 2004: 39

2004: 25, 26, 33)? As for the focus groups, the 'general consensus' is that: 'students and residents do not mix socially, and do not have adequate social facilities; and Hatfield lacks the vitality of a university town, has inadequate infrastructure, and has an unsafe town centre' (PACEC 2004: 36).

Upsides and downsides are brought together in an intriguing diagrammatic form (see Figure 9.10).

Collectively, the Cambridge and Hertfordshire data raise another important question. What are the activities which the university should support in the interests of community engagement? Higher education institutions are not funded as an alternative set of social or recreational services. They have to husband their resources to support their core purposes. However, in all of the cases above (including the Hertfordshire bus service) it is possible to construct an audit trail back to what the university is there to do (in this case, get its members to work safely, efficiently and with the least possible negative influence on the environment). In terms of the Cambridge objectives, this confirms the centrality of 'leading to new opportunities in teaching and research'.

On the face of things, priorities like these *are* recognized in public discourse, as set out in Chapter 3. However, the inescapable dilemma is that community–university interaction is going to be even less structured around the linear model of knowledge transfer and exchange than university–business interaction, as the University of Minnesota typology (discussed at the end of Chapter 4) attests. To work well, in twenty-first-century conditions, it is going to be dependent on what William James (1981: 462) called 'a blooming, buzzing confusion' of dialogue on in the increasingly permeable boundary between modern universities and their communities. Messages will go both ways. There will be abortive as well as highly successful projects (this is a riskier domain than designing a better mouse-trap – another American philosophical reference). Circumstances and conditions will change. But, if we are going to have higher education playing a fully engaged role in today's civil society, we are going to have to make this work.

# 10

# MANAGING CIVIC ENGAGEMENT: OUTSIDE THE ACADEMY

*While members, and especially leaders, of HEIs look out, others look in. This chapter concludes with discussion of the special challenges of managing the resulting external relationships to best effect. However, it is necessary first to tackle a broader question: in whose interest is it that universities and colleges should succeed in their civic and community engagement? Some of the answers to this question are then tested in a contentious area of public policy: the case of equity and diversity of student participation.*

## Higher education and the public interest

It has become fashionable again to talk about higher education and the public interest. I have noted above how in England, HEFCE has added 'securing the public interest' to the objectives in its latest strategic plan (HEFCE 2006). What exactly does this mean; what should it mean?

Sometimes the relevant discourse is critical. In 2004 Robert Reich gave a high octane lecture for the Higher Education Policy Institute (HEPI). In his words:

> generally there has been a decline ... in the mission of public education. Instead of a public investment for a public return, instead of the rationale being to mobilise the most talented members of society for the good of society, for social leadership in a more complex world – the kind of rhetoric we heard in the 1950s, '60s and early 1970s – the emphasis has shifted.
>
> (Reich 2004: 5)

In his view these honourable objectives have been swamped by the more brittle concepts of human capital and of atomized meritocracy (Reich 2004). In contrast the triumphalist tendency turns Reich's vices into virtues, as in all of those official documents which associate the work of higher education with the growth of GDP, as well as with graduate rates of return on their (and their families') 'investment' in the higher education product.

One consequence is that we are in one of those periods where university introspection is matched by a strident debate about what use universities are anyway ('what have the universities ever done for us?'). We can say 'one of those periods' because we have been there before: in early fourteenth-century Paris; in mid-nineteenth-century America; in late nineteenth-century Germany and in mid-twentieth-century Britain.

What *is* the role of the HE sector in these circumstances? The basic answer is twofold. We can clarify some of the questions, as well as the basis on which they can be responsibly answered. That is a contribution to the external context. And we can help to put our own house in order, including through disciplined self-study. That is about our 'internal' obligations, and was covered in the previous chapter. Other questions follow naturally.

Question one: *how do we establish the public interest?* It is not the same as the interest of the state, and it is certainly not the interest of the government of the day. Look around the world at the contexts where universities are co-opted into national, or sectional, or even ethnic crusades. Early results from a 15-country project on 'the role of universities in the transformation of societies' would urge caution on the more aggressive advocates of higher education and the national interest. The authors find, in general, a 'relatively weak' role for HE in stimulating economic change, 'complex and contradictory' influence on political change, and a social role that is at least as much about reproduction as about transformation (Brennan *et al.* 2004: 8).

Question two: *where does the university sit in civil society?* Civil society is now a rather old-fashioned concept, as in the famous Thatcher/Kinnock stand-off, 'is there such a thing as society?' According to Michael Edwards of the Ford Foundation, 'as a concept' civil society 'speaks to the best of us, and calls upon the best of us to respond in kind' (Edwards 2004: iii; see also Delanty 2001: 5–10, and Slowey and Watson 2003: 135–51). As for the university in this context: is it a microcosm; an entirely autonomous agent; a service agency; or a social sorting device? Where does the notion of 'public benefit' play into all of this?

Question three: *how does the university work?* Think about the contradictory pressures the university or college is under, as discussed in the Introduction (Chapter 1). Does it lead or lag? Is it part of the solution to our social and economic ills or part of the problem? Who do universities work for, when they are not working for themselves (that is, creating the next generation of scholars in particular disciplines and professions)? The answer has changed over time. However, in the early twenty-first century, the answer is clear. British higher education is working for the National Health Service (NHS) (or more broadly for the health and social care industry). Our exposure is staggering. Health and social care now account for 14 per cent of our student numbers, 19 per cent of our fees and 30 per cent of our research income (UUK 2004b).

Question four: *who belongs to the university, and to whom does the university belong?* Newman said that the university should know 'all her children, one by one'. Are our students customers, clients or members? There's much talk about *stakeholders* these days, but what exactly is a stakeholder? 'Stakeholder', like 'client' is one of those words which has almost exactly the opposite meaning from when it was originally coined (Appiah notes how 'client' and 'patron' have switched roles in the power game – 'the client is now ... the boss' – Appiah 2006: 93). The stakeholder used to be the person who held the coats – and the prize-money – while the fight was on; the notion was one of scrupulous disinterest. As discussed in the next chapter, stakeholders need to understand that if they are to live up to the modern designation (as having invested something themselves), they have to put something at risk. Otherwise they simply support the cynical public sector manager's definition of a stakeholder as 'someone who can do you harm'. (Mike Fitzgerald, the former Vice-Chancellor of Thames Valley University, used to say that every time he heard the word he had an image of Dracula rising from his coffin.)

Question five: *what is the university for?* What is the effect of society having universities or colleges, rather than any other centre of knowledge production and use? Is it benign (as in the 'wider benefits of learning' (WBL) analysis – which has securely established how graduates are not only wealthier, but also happier, healthier, and more democratically tolerant than their non-graduate peers) or toxic? (See Bynner *et al.* 2003; Schuller *et al.* 2004.)

The answers to all these questions have implications for the world of public policy in which universities play a part, and hence for the type of civic engagement that is possible as well as desirable.

## The case of widening participation

A 'public discourse' analysis would probably reveal that 'widening participation' (WP) is the most troublesome item in talk about higher education; in the media, in politics and beyond. Its record in creating 'moral panic' (as in the Laura Spence affair or in aspects of the Second Reading debate on the 2004 Higher Education Bill) is notorious. Second on this list probably comes 'employability' as a code for what students should want and employers say they are not getting; and third 'dumbing-down' in all its manifestations (entry standards, 'Mickey Mouse' courses, 'grade-inflation', and so on).

Talking about widening participation is, however, not the same as thinking about it, and these three fields of contention share another characteristic: that the related research field is so cluttered with non-commensurate, non-replicable research that anyone with a strongly held opinion can find a research study to back it up.

There is also code in the WP arena. It can get bound up in discussions about 'social engineering' and 'meritocracy' in the wider society. It can be prayed in aid by colleges and institutions which feel disadvantaged by competitive approaches to resourcing (especially research). As demonstrated in Chapter 3, it could be said to have derailed the UK government's attempts to improve the funding of universities, as the debates over the 2003 White Paper and 2004 Higher Education bill shifted (as they invariably do) from questions about how to fund institutions to questions about how to support students.

## Why does widening participation matter?

At its heart, of course, widening participation is an issue of social justice. More concretely, succeeding at it contributes to social cohesion. The iron law seems to be that if you want higher education to be fairer, you have to allow it to expand. As you allow it to expand, you also have to consider the position of those who do not participate.

The more successful that national systems are in growing participation and achievement, the greater will be the gap between those who stay on a ladder of educational attainment and those who drop off. In the UK we have solid, longitudinal data about the positive effects of participation not only on the economic status of the individual beneficiary (in terms of HE the current government's almost exclusive selling point for its reforms), but also on their health and happiness and, democratic engagement and tolerance; to say nothing of the life chances of their children.

In the mean time, we have a lot of international hand-wringing about 'completion', 'persistence', or 'retention' (as well as their reciprocals, 'drop out' and 'wastage'). But the big picture is that we do not talk enough about 're-starting' or 're-engagement'.

The most important issue is the growing gulf between a successful majority and a disengaged minority. This becomes even more dangerous as, in the words of Stephen Gorard and his team's comprehensive report on the results of widening participation research to the HEFCE, 'the culture of HE/FE has merged with mainstream culture' (Gorard *et al.* 2006: 12). The permanently disengaged become the individual 'self-blamers' whose histories have been eloquently mapped by Karen Evans and others (Evans 2003); collectively they make up what Ferdinand Mount calls the newly discovered class of 'downers' (Mount 2004).

There are serious issues here for social mobility. Is HE simply a sorting device or does it have transformative possibilities? Unless it begins to deliver the latter, its social effects will be regressive. Gorard refers throughout to the problem of the 'usual suspects'. In another recent report Nigel Brown and his collaborators have mapped the territory as it affects young adults. Their title gives away the story: *Breaking Out of the Silos: 14–30 Education and Skills Policy* (Brown *et al.* 2004). What Brown *et al.* call the 'royal route' (5+ good GCSEs, 2+ A levels, followed by a full-time degree) dominates patterns of aspiration as well as of analysis (Brown *et al.* 2004: 14). It is also worthy of note that the royal route invariably leads away from home, with a direct correlation between A-level achievement and distance travelled to study (Gorard *et al.* 2006: 116).

Hence Alison Wolf's devastating description of vocational education as being 'a great idea for other people's children' (Wolf 2003: 56). Hence also the battles over 'fair access' to HE (and the accusations of 'social engineering' – which has become almost as universal an epithet in contemporary British political discourse as 'liberal' in the USA). Gorard identifies the exact opposite of the 'royal route' for those from multiply disadvantaged backgrounds: limited educational chances and achievement, higher prospects of dropping out at all stages, and – if you do make it all the way through to graduation – lower earnings prospects and higher debt.

## What do we mean by widening participation?

Widening participation can be a *portmanteau* concept. Here is how it is defined by the Economic and Social Research Council (ESRC) Teaching and Learning Research Programme (TLRP) in describing the set of projects they have recently commissioned:

Widening participation is taken to mean extending and enhancing access to HE experiences of people from so-called underrepresented and diverse subject backgrounds, families, groups and communities and positively enabling such people to participate in and benefit from HE. People from socially disadvantaged families and/or deprived geographical areas, including deprived remote, rural and coastal areas or from families that have no prior experience of HE may be of key concern. Widening participation is also concerned with diversity in terms of ethnicity, gender, disability and social background in particular HE disciplines, modes and institutions. It can also include access and participation across the ages, extending conceptions of learning across the life-course, and in relation to family responsibilities, particularly by gender and maturity (for details on the seven 'WP' projects currently supported by the TLRP see www.tlrp.org).

So that is the researchers' view of the field. It does not omit much. The basic point is that widening participation is not just, or even primarily, about minorities. The equation of (class) × (gender) × (ethnicity) × (age) × (location) is a very complex one, and is now being added to by newly prominent variables such as disability. In the USA and the UK, for example, the position of poor young white males is now recognized as one of the most intractable problems (Jones 2005). Meanwhile for the 'perfect storm' concatenation of indicators of educational deprivation, look at the prospects of the group of what are now optimistically called 'cared-for' children (Jackson *et al.* 2005).

## How are we (the UK and England in particular) doing?

International benchmarking is notoriously difficult in this, as in many other, educational settings. As indicated in the discussion of the student experience in Chapter 9, a dimension we rarely tackle is the comparison of participation indices across the European Union. It is interesting to reflect on how this pattern may be changed by the 'accession' states (and some useful preliminary work has been done by the Higher Education Policy Institute – HEPI 2004a). In the mean time, it is worth reflecting on why (despite all of our legitimate concerns about equity), the UK seems to do comparatively well. Looking from the USA to the UK, the latter may seem less diverse and more fixed into a traditional mould. Looking from the UK to Europe puts everything in an entirely different light.

A question which elides the empirical and the normative is that of *ambition.* By international standards the UK is doing well at some extremely important aspects of HE (research, retention, the global market, and so on). We are also doing well at lifelong learning (including CPD) for those members of society who remain engaged. We are doing less well in the immediate post-compulsory area, and this is where the fork in the road between the engaged and the disengaged appears to be located.

This is largely because of where this particular sector starts in the UK: at 16 formally, and at about 14 informally with the increasing evidence of disaffection in schools. What we know is that the 'participation gain' generated by the much needed reform of the 16+ examination system is probably now exhausted (Ashton 2003). Essentially we have created a fault-line between those who succeed and those who fail post-16 because we are scared of the alternative: that of declaring that nobody's publicly supported education and training should cease at 16. In many competitor economies employing 16-year-olds without offering education and training would not only be unthinkable but also illegal. In her 1997 report *Learning Works* (FEFC 1997), Helena Kennedy was adamant that the threshold level for subsequent happier and more productive lives stands at Level 3, not Level 2. If we want a high-added value, knowledge-based, globally competitive economy, we should understand that it is incompatible with maintaining what is called 'the youth labour market'.

This raises another set of performance questions: access to what, and with what effect on life chances? Gorard points out how little effect the WP agenda has had in 'changing the product' within HE itself. There is no recent worked example that can match the undoubted emancipatory impact on earlier generations of either the London University external degree or the Open University.

As for life chances after graduation, the Council for Industry and Higher Education, among others have pointed out that employers have been notoriously slow to appreciate the benefits of a wider and more inclusive pool of graduates (CIHE 2002).

## What works (here and elsewhere)?

The English Higher Education Act of 2004 put the concept of 'under-represented groups' on the face of legislation for the first time. While undoubtedly well-meaning, this may turn out to be a dangerous development. The notion of a political majority deciding at any time who is and who is not most 'under-represented', for the purposes of selective help, should chill the blood.

A survey of the fate of what might be regarded as 'under-represented groups' around the world will show what I mean. Turn the question on its head, and look at local cultural and political hang-ups. Who, in fact, is meant to be left outside? The experience of other countries is that targeted positive discrimination invariably has unintended knock-on effects. Examples have included the physically disabled in China, the Chinese ethnic minority in Pacific Rim countries, Israeli Arabs, Hungarian Romanies, and the relatives of terrorists in Japan (see Watson 2005b: 137).

To look through the other end of the telescope, how much should a university try to look like its host community? How important is this as an institutional and/or a sectoral priority? How, in enrolling and developing students from across the current groups in society, can the university or college seek to change that community for the better?

In the USA, elite universities compete for excellent students from minorities and from disadvantaged communities because they are trying to construct a 'class' which will be representative of the best and brightest that American society can offer in the future (there is an element of self-interest here too) (Bowen *et al.* 2005). In Great Britain the discourse is structured much more around a 'deficit' model, agonizing about the 'under-representation' of lower socio-economic groups in particular in the system as a whole, and especially in the more prestigious institutions.

In both countries this has become a contentious issue, as American institutions move their financial aid resources away from 'need' and towards 'merit' (scholarly and athletic), and as UK institutions tackle the unwelcome fact that the conventionally qualified students from poorer backgrounds are just not there in sufficient numbers to satisfy the political critics (Wickenden 2006). In both countries there is a dearth of clear thinking about the empirical bases of the argument, partly because of the lack of really solid longitudinal, controlled evidence about the motivation, assets and characteristics of the actual and potential 'market'. This is the big message in the Gorard report: we do not really know what we think we know.

## What is to be done?

As in most 'moral panic' circumstances, we can see an almost pathetic search for the single-issue intervention that will improve the situation (often without consideration of knock-on effects), and a similarly dysfunctional search for scapegoats (someone else to blame).

Closer investigation will reveal that many such prejudices are irrational, and that many conclusions arising from systematic research are counter-intuitive. For example, in the UK it is increasingly clear that widening participation is *not* about the following (at least to the extent that is often claimed.

Widening participation is not about consistently perverse decisions by higher education admissions tutors. Especially in some universities, these gatekeepers can be pompous, narrow and seriously uninformed. But such *traits* have not created the system. If anything, says Gorard, university admissions have improved rather than further undermined distributional fairness (Gorard *et al.* 2006: 41). A recent study by the Nuffield Foundation's 14–19 group showed how hard well-motivated admissions tutors do try – across the system – although this carefully nuanced report played all too predictably in the press as another 'moral panic' (see Wilde *et al.* 2006, and then the *Times Higher Educational Supplement*'s lead story 'Tutors in despair at illiterate freshers', 10 February 2006).

Meanwhile, advocates and opponents of a post-qualifications admissions (PQA) system add another variety of 'single-issue' debate. Whatever the merits of getting rid of the system of 'conditional offers' might be, it is not at all clear that the main benefits would be felt by well-qualified, socially disadvantaged students doing better in examinations than either they or their teachers predict. (Another boomlet, referred to by Gorard *et al.*, is tied up in the argument for random distribution of places. This is highly unlikely to persuade the Headmasters' Conference.)

Nor is WP about well-qualified students from poorer or minority backgrounds making irrational choices of institution. This is one of several mistakes made by Stephen Schwarz in his two sadly unimaginative reports on higher education admissions (DfES 2004a, 2004b). In these 'fairness' is related to 'equal opportunity for all individuals, regardless of background to gain admission to a course suited to their ability and background' (DfES 2004a: 4.1); that is, it is not about a simple competition which some will win and some will lose. Instead it assumes (absurdly) that if everybody behaves appropriately, the number and quality of the places available will match the number and quality of the applicants (the *Guardian*'s Guy Browning said 'the trouble with fairness is that there isn't enough to go around' – Browning 2004). Genuinely 'fairer admissions' will involve telling some apparently well-qualified students (especially those whose families have spent a lot of disposable income making them so) why they have *not* been selected. Meanwhile reassurance will be required for well-qualified students from poorer backgrounds that going to an institution other than 'the most selective' can be a life-affirming choice. For some students pharmacy at Bradford, or fashion textiles at Brighton, will make a lot more sense – in academic, as well as career and 'networking' terms – than medicine at Oxford, or history of art at Exeter.

Above all there is the question of how many such students there are. Bahram Bekhradnia and others have consistently reminded us how high A-level grades also correlate with family prosperity (Foxwood 2006: 142). In this sense, the problem of raising aspiration, or 'fair access' to prestigious institutions is a tiny one compared with the genuine WP challenge of getting more people to the matriculation starting gate.

Widening participation is not always about lack of 'aspiration' by those whose compulsory schooling has taken a wrong turn (or even a rational turn into vocational routes). There is not enough research on the real feelings and capabilities of the non-engaged. Gorard points out how quickly most studies simply focus on the players rather than the non-players, who are relegated to a passive and silent background role. What this can disguise is how many of them are not passive by choice, but seriously angry about the hand they have been dealt (see Gorard *et al.* 2006: 32; Slowey and Watson 2003: xix–xx).

Widening participation is not about simple debt aversion. As suggested in the previous chapter, we need to look at attitudes to debt in the wider, young population.

Widening participation is not simply about supply-side issues, such as the lack of short-cycle alternatives to traditional degrees, even though the latter can be most popular magic bullets. It is not clear that the latest such experiment – the foundation degree – will prove any more successful than its predecessor the Diploma in Higher Education (DipHE), introduced in the 1970s. Certainly the propensity for its greatest take-up to be among public service 'uniforms' – health workers, classroom assistants, the police and the armed forces – seems very reminiscent of the way in which the DipHE rapidly became the normal initial qualification for nurses.

In fact there is no silver bullet in prospect by fixing any of these. At the same time, the evidence is increasingly clear (and hard to live with) that the following interventions would help.

Widening participation in the UK *is* potentially about improving the quality of school-based experience for all students, but especially those from under-represented groups. Success in compulsory education is vital. What is more, you do not get this by separating sheep from goats, whether or not the pens are labelled 'academic' and 'vocational' or 'public' and 'private'. This goes to the heart of national ambition, and, again as set out above, I think that the UK is seriously wanting in this respect, including most recently in the political response to the Tomlinson Report on reform of qualifications for 14–19-year-olds.

Widening participation *is* about parental expectations; and there is a danger in the current cross-party consensus that giving more 'power to the parents' who are already powerful is likely to increase rather than reduce polarization. This is not to say that poorer parents do not want 'choice', just that it is notoriously harder for the system to supply it. However, Gorard points to the higher than average positive influence of parents from some ethnic minorities (Gorard *et al.* 2006: 98).

Widening participation *is* about governments and employers recognizing that Level 3 (high school graduation in international terms, or university matriculation in UK-speak) is, as suggested above, the pivot, or tipping point, for the creation of a learning society.

Perhaps most importantly it is about getting employers to live up to their rhetoric of supporting both younger and older workers in the personal learning trajectories (especially the former). The quarter of all English 16–18-year-olds who are receiving no education and training at all, even when in work, all too easily converts into the one-third of all adults who engage in no further learning at all after the school-leaving age (NCE 2003: 11; Gorard *et al.* 2006: 5).

There are some genuinely 'wicked issues' here for a sector – and for institutions – concerned with fairness and social justice. One is the tension between expansion and participation. As set out above, to achieve increased 'fairness' will require further expansion, but at the same time it risks increasingly disadvantaging those who do not participate. And so there are difficulties in working out how to help the disadvantaged without further advantaging the advantaged. At the practical level, there are further difficulties with targeted interventions that end up by undermining and confusing each other.

Finally, on this track, we have a problem about lack of patience. The solutions here (including critically growing a broader base in society that will have confidence in mass or universal higher education because it has experience of it) are inevitably long term.

This is not to say that from the perspective of the university or college, 'fair access' and 'widening participation' are somebody else's problems. Indeed this might be said to be a test case of how far the higher education system is genuinely inside and implicated in the success of civil society, rather than apart and downstream from its day-to-day dilemmas. Higher education cannot tackle this problem by itself; equally it cannot simply say that it is somebody else's job.

In this context, we must accept (and respond to) the fact that British institutions can be hard-wired to resist this aspect of civic and community engagement. A classic problem is the 'header tank' on admissions, whereby institutions recruit first the students whom it easiest to recruit and then go looking for the rest. Another is our reluctance, inside universities and colleges, to make constructive use of credit accumulation and transfer (as opposed to devising frameworks used for accumulation, but rarely for transfer – HEPI 2004b). A third is the tendency to over-hype ICT-based solutions to almost any pedagogical challenge (in relation to WP, Gorard takes this as a 'case-study' – Gorard *et al.* 2006: 13–17).

The sector and its representatives have also been slow to lead the relevant public policy debate. On the latter point, as in the USA, we seem to have here a set of priorities that institutional leaders discover when they are about to retire (Broers 2005).

Under instruction from government, HEFCE is, of course, under almost permanent pressure to do more. To return to the Secretary of State's 2006 letter (introduced in Chapter 3), the relevant paragraph reads as follows:

> The second [priority] is on widening participation in HE for low income families, where in spite of the recent progress we have made we do not perform well enough. Low rates of participation in HE among the lowest socio-economic groups represent entrenched inequality and in economic terms a waste of human capital. I [the Secretary of State] am therefore asking the Council to explore options for additional support in widening participation in 2006–07, building on the work that has already been done in understanding the costs to institutions.
>
> (Ruth Kelly to David Young, 31 January 2006)

The interesting point here is the selection of indicators, interventions, and levers. The political focus is on income (as a proxy for class?), on human capital formation, and on responding to a case made by the Council for additional teaching funding support (to improve targeted recruitment and subsequent retention). These are all worthy and rational causes, but they may serve to disguise other variables: other forms of discrimination; the social capital effects; and the inadequacy of core institutional support. In other words, the dialogue about a 'compact' (Chapter 3) needs to be revived.

## Managing civic engagement: 'outside-in' perspectives

The list of civic and community engagement possibilities set out in the previous chapter can, of course, all be viewed from through the other end of the telescope. In so far as they all depend upon structured partnerships with individuals, agencies and organizations outside the academy they represent *relationships* which have to be managed.

Some of these will be *political* – at the national, regional and local level. Others will be *professional* – with professional bodies, with businesses and other institutions, individually and collectively. A particularly important subset will be with the voluntary and charitable sector. Yet others will be *personal*, serendipitous and opportunistic.

Critical to making all these relationships work (as set out in the results of benchmarking in Chapter 7) are the terms of trade. Robinson and Katalushi set out a list of 'significant others', or, as they call them, 'stakeholders', without critically examining what will make all of these relationships idiosyncratic, or at least different (see the discussion of stakeholders in Chapter 11).

- national and local government;
- community organizations;
- other funding bodies;
- industry and professions;
- undergraduates and postgraduates;
- teachers and researchers;
- student support services;
- student union;
- trade unions;
- society as a whole (Robinson and Katalushi 2005: 260).

The most sensitive set of external relationships, absent from this analysis, is likely to be with other HEIs, especially in the same city or the same region. Here all the official rhetoric is about cooperation, collaboration and complementarity. The reality is likely to be different, with rivalry, resentment and lack of mutual respect not far beneath the surface. At its best, coordinated higher education planning can deliver the following:

- shared projects and collaborative provision;
- a 'pre-competitive' response to needs articulated by the community;

- joint representation on the myriad working groups and standing committees which local and regional authorities set up; and
- as close to a single higher education voice as is possible to requests for advice.

Figure 10.1, as a worked example, is how the mix has played out for the Universities of Brighton and Sussex.

Beyond the Medical School, which opened in 2003, probably the most high-profile example of collaboration (involving higher education partners in addition to the two universities) is the University Centre Hastings (UCH), formally opened by the then Minister for Higher Education Alan Johnson in January 2004.

Communities lacking universities up and down the country are accustomed to see a higher education foundation as the key to prosperity and prestige. Creating new institutions is, however, a long, hard, and not immediately satisfying prospect (MacLeod and Curtis 2004). University Centre Hastings sought to break the mould. This is how the Minister was briefed:

---

Background information

- Hastings needs help. Overall it is the 27th most deprived English district and, educationally, census data shows it is 292/376 in England/Wales for qualifications at degree level or higher, while regionally it is 3/67 for adults with no qualification.
- The Hastings and Bexhill Regeneration Plan identifies education as one of its five focus areas.
- The UCH concept was proposed by the University of Brighton as a means of rapidly developing a high quality higher education component to the education strategy. It builds on the University's historical connections with both with Hastings College of Arts and Technology (HCAT) and the Conquest Hospital, as well as other established HE interests in the town of the University of Sussex's Centre for Continuing Education and the Open University. An early milestone was achieved in September 2003 with the enrolment of over 400 HE students on franchised courses.
- The 'Coastal Highway' (a collaborative project between all of the HEIs in Sussex) has piloted early intervention in local secondary schools, raising aspiration for further and higher education. This has now been developed under 'Partnerships for Progression' (P4P) and will thereby cover all secondary schools in Hastings.

---

*Figure 10.1* Universities of Brighton and Sussex: collaborative activities

**Major partnerships**
- The Brighton & Sussex Medical School
- Dental School bid (failed)
- The Freeman Centre (Science Policy Research Unit – SPRU and Centre for Research into Innovation Management – CENTRIM)
- Qualifying courses in Social Work
- Some taught postgraduate courses
- The Sussex Liaison and Progression Accord*
- Aimhigher*
- Reciprocal library membership
- Reciprocal fee waivers for staff
- Local Area Network (LENS)*
- Reciprocal (co-opted) membership of the Board and Council

(* includes other academic partners)

**University of Brighton lead**
- University Centre Hastings (UCH)
- The Sussex Learning Network (Lifelong Learning Network)
- The Community–University Knowledge Exchange (HEIF 2)
- The Community–University Partnership Programme (CUPP)
- The Coastal Highway (WP project)

**University of Sussex lead**
- Creativity in Engineering (Centre of Excellence in Teaching & Learning)
- Foundation degree for community leaders

**Earlier initiatives (now wound up)**
- The Sussex Technology Institute (1990–92)
- The Sussex Innovation Centre (partners bought out by the University of Sussex 2003)
- The Sussex Academic Corridor
- COPS (ESRC Centre on 'Complex Products')

**Joint representation**
- The Brighton & Hove City Board
- The Brighton & Hove Children's Trust
- Strategic Health Authorities
- Various business and educational groups throughout the region

**'Shared intelligence'**
- The 'Joint Planning Group' (meets termly)
- Fees, bursaries and student support
- Private sector student housing
- Public relations issues

**Many informal links in research and community engagement**

- The initial facility is a building refurbished through SEEDA's (SEEDA is the South East England Development Agency) capital support. The University of Brighton has successfully bid to HEFCE's Strategic Development Fund for both capital and revenue support, and also achieved commitments in principle to the award of additional student numbers (ASNs).
- The Sussex LSC has just completed a 16–19 review with a major series of recommendations for changes in secondary education.

Why UCH is important

- UCH offers the prospect for education-led regeneration initially by meeting the growing demand in the Hastings and Bexhill area, where participation rates are below average, then attracting students from across the region, and eventually nationally and internationally.
- The approach is novel in that it creates a 'serviced' university facility under the management of the University of Brighton where HE providers can offer courses. Current partners are Universities of Brighton and Sussex, the OU [Open University], HCAT and Canterbury Christ Church University College.
- The governance is also unique in that each HEI is responsible for the quality and delivery of its own courses while a management committee (chaired by the University of Brighton) brings together the functioning requirements of UCH, and a stakeholders group (chaired by SEEDA) provides linkage with the local and regional stakeholders and employer needs.

The future

- UCH will continue with its current business/IT focus and quickly initiate courses in education/health and social care with foundation degrees and undergraduate degrees in business, humanities and eventually the life sciences. Continuing professional development (CPD) will also be an important priority. This will start in health, where there is an existing base and demand, and expand quickly into the business area linking together the third stream activities of both HE and FE [further education].
- SEEDA, through its own contacts, is exploring a number of other education initiatives that could extend the range of partners and use of the facilities.

- Within four to five years it is expected that demand will fill the building and it is proposed to move to a new purpose built facility close by on the Station Plaza development site.
- The Learning and Skills Council is also anticipating a substantial capital programme as it reorganises 16 to 19 provision, which will provide a further stimulus to participation as well as offer the possibility for joint sharing of resources such as learning resource centres and computing facilities.
- Eventually the HE focus will lead to the development of both academic and industrially based research activities as a major contribution to the regeneration of the town.

There are several useful lessons here:

- the need to overcome regional stereotyping (Hastings – and other coastal towns are black spots on the image of a prosperous South East);
- the value of rapid response (most of the new public money going into HE had been earmarked for a bypass scheme; when this was turned down a coalition of partners, including higher education, ensured that the resource was not lost to the community);
- the power of partnership (for there to have been a 'winner-takes-all' competition for establishing the new campus, would – as it has elsewhere – have considerably delayed the process);
- the promotional value of declaring small victories on a regular basis (this has been a serious part of keeping UCH in the news: the first 400 HE students in the town; opening a new learning resources centre; the first Hastings-based graduates; the arrival of new partners; and so on); and
- that HEIs, under the right circumstances are perfectly capable of acting boldly, and taking risks (the University of Brighton, for example, was prepared to put its university title on the line).

To take an example from the other end of the country, the creation of a Science City in Newcastle-on-Tyne, demonstrates a similar set of public and private partnerships, but in this from a narrower HE institutional base. 'Science Cities' were pre-figured in both the Lambert Review and the government's Science and Innovation Strategy (Lambert 2003; HMT/DTI/DfES 2004). Newcastle, York and Manchester were designated in the November 2004 budget statement, and Birmingham, Nottingham and Bristol added in the Budget itself in March 2005. Newcastle is probably the most fully worked example, involving Newcastle University, a 19-acre city-centre facility called Science Central, and other offshoots like a 'campus for Ageing and Vitality' (on a refurbished hospital site). The absentees from significant participation and investment are the other significant HEIs in the city and the region (Bennewith and Dawley 2006).

Many of the difficulties here relate to *representation*. Who, for the purposes of civic and community engagement *is* the university, and who the community? Getting this wrong – miscalculating the level or the comprehensiveness of the representation – can be profoundly dysfunctional. Institutional leaders, in particular are supposed to have (or very quickly to grow) regional or community roots and loyalties. Such loyalty is hard, and runs the risk of seeming insincere if it is transferred quickly or aggressively. 'Eating for the university' is an art, sometimes painfully acquired. In the other direction, there is the danger of the community playing out some of its own tensions and splits (look what happens when local authorities change, or as is frequently the case recently, lose overall political control) with or across the university.

Above all, as indicated in the previous chapter, and further explored in the next, there is an irreducible moral dimension to the dialogue. The University of Bristol has recently re-branded its Public Programmes Office (formerly the Department of Continuing Education) as the Centre for Public Engagement (see www.bris.ac.uk/cms/cpe). Why? Here is a revealing vignette from Eric Thomas, the Vice-Chancellor:

> I should highlight that universities are part of the moral and intellectual agenda in their city ... A good example is our involvement in Brunel 200, which was a big local celebration of the 200th anniversary of Brunel's birth. Of course we put on lectures about Brunel as an engineer and about engineering in general. But Brunel was also the son of a migrant, and we have also developed a series of public lectures later this year to discuss migration and diversity in a community at the beginning of the 21st century. That was done deliberately because we believed there were very unsettling pronouncements about this being made in many parts of the society and that it was important to publicly address the issue.
>
> (Keynote speech to HECP conference,
> Birkbeck College, 7 July 2006)

# 11

# THE UNIVERSITY COMMUNITY IN THE COMMUNITY

*It has been a recurrent theme of this book that, in order to act effectively in the civic and community arena, a university or college needs to know and understand itself, at a deep and satisfying level. This final chapter explores the dimensions of such self-knowledge, and concludes on a rather old-fashioned note, with a defence of the 'liberal' concept of higher education.*

## Forms of engagement

To step back initially from the fray, university 'civic engagement' can be described in three domains: first, second and third order.

In this account *first-order engagement* arises from the university just being there. One of the primary roles for universities is to produce graduates who go to work (perhaps in areas completely unconnected with those they have studied); who play their parts in civil society (where the evidence suggests they are likely to contribute more wisdom and tolerance than if they had not been to university); who have families (and read to their children); who pay their taxes (and return a proportion of their higher-than-average incomes as graduates through progressive taxation); and who (increasingly) support 'their' universities, through gifts and legacies.

Also in this domain, universities guard treasures (real and virtual), in their museums, galleries and archives. They provide a safe place for the exploration of difficult issues or challenging ideas (Melvyn Bragg, Chancellor of the University of Leeds, describes universities as 'the water cooler around which is gathered arguments about the society we want to be' – Robinson and Katalushi 2005: viii–ix).

They also supply material for a branch of popular culture (the campus novel, film and television series). Incidentally, like the best art, this genre sometimes leads and sometimes follows. Departments of Elvis Studies or Hitler Studies did not exist before Don De Lillo called them into being, while David Lodge had to preface *Thinks*, his latest campus novel with the epigram: 'The University of Gloucester is a fictional construct: at least it was at the time of writing.' A couple of decades earlier he similarly founded the University of Limerick. For more on all of this see Elaine Showalter (2005: *passim*). Of course, not all of the outcomes are humorous. Tom Wolfe's Candide-like evocation of Duke University in *I Am Charlotte Simmons*, preceded the scandals of 2006 surrounding a varsity athletic team whose celebrations went appallingly wrong (Wolfe 2004; Boyer 2006).

Together these features add resonance to the university as a social institution in its own right: at its best a model of continuity and a focus of aspiration for a better and more fulfilled life; at its worst a source of envy and resentment. Understanding this first order relationship between universities and their communities provides an insight into the cultural role of universities and colleges in different national contexts: in the USA they are more loved and respected than they deserve; in Australia and the UK they stimulate more opprobrium than is objectively fair. This picture may, however, be changing, as US higher education is hitting – almost for the first time – a combination of cuts in public subsidy, consumer resentment and consumer debt.

'First order' considerations also imply that universities should strive to behave well; to be ethical beacons. In the words of Derek Bok, 'the university reveals its own ethical standards in many ways, including its scrupulousness in upholding academic standards, its decency and fairness in dealing with students and employees, and its sensitivity in relating to the community in which it resides' (Bok 2006: 160). It is no accident that Simon Robinson and Clement Katalushi conclude their account of *Values in Higher Education* with an appeal to 'integrity', following Robert Solomon's definition of 'a complex of virtues, working together to form a coherent character, an identifiable and trustworthy personality' (Robinson and Katalushi 2005: 263). 'Integrity' is also the core concept for Jon Nixon in his account of how the three pillars of academic practice support each other.

> Research, scholarship and teaching do not simply hang together instrumentally. They are dependent upon and at the same time help to sustain a moral framework, the pivotal points of which are truthfulness (accuracy/sincerity), respect (attentiveness/

honesty) and authenticity (courage/compassion). The university
viewed as a 'utopian state' ... is a civic space within which these
particular virtues, and the dispositions associated with them, are
allowed to flourish.

(Nixon 2004: 251)

This is not how universities and colleges are invariably seen. As
institutions they can behave badly as well as behaving well. Some
examples of 'bad behaviour' include the following. They can offer
misleading promotion and advice, to staff, students and potential
students, about their real performance and intentions. As powerful
institutions they can undermine and intimidate their members, their
partners and their clients. They can perpetuate self-serving myths.
They can hide behind specious arguments (narrow constructions of
'academic freedom', *force majeure*, and the like). They can displace
responsibilities (and blame others). They can fail the 'stewardship
test' (for example, by not assessing and responding to risk, or by
cutting corners, or by 'letting go'). They can be bad neighbours. At
their worst they can be simply corrupt (the Observatory on Higher
Education has a current project on 'corruption'). Above all, they can
fail to tell the truth to themselves as least as easily as failing to tell
truth to power. (See, for a poignant example of an institution
struggling to come to terms with its past, the initiative led by Ruth
Simmons, the first African-American President of an Ivy League
university, to help Brown University to acknowledge its founders'
role in the slave trade – Fitzgerald 2005; Van Der Werf 2006.)

Perhaps it is this failure of reflexivity, of scholarly self-knowledge,
which is most surprising, and can be most reprehensible. There is a
major paradox in terms of the lack of penetration of these theoretical
and analytical perspectives into higher education itself, which
otherwise would pride itself on being a source of objective critique.
Academics on academia, as opposed to academics within their subjects, seem depressingly incapable of either theoretical self-
knowledge or empirical understanding of their role and that of their
institutions within a wider society. Regular pathologies include the
following: blind spots and selective memory (for example, most
members of the academic community would now regard the UK
Open University as one of their most distinctive contributions – at
the time of its birth they fought it tooth and nail); a curious kind of
hyperbolic internal populism (as in the doomed attack on external
peer review of teaching and research quality over the past decade and
a half); and a kind of naive detachment (as in controversies over
grants and fees). As Gordon Graham concludes, 'when it comes to
debates and disagreements about their own affairs, universities are as

prone to self-protecting flights of unreason as any other institution' (Graham 2005: 280). Meanwhile, there are also temptations here for celebrity vice-chancellors. Do institutional leaders have to prove their entrepreneurial credentials by encouraging their colleagues to behave badly? It sometimes feels so.

To return to the crisis of conscience in American higher education, this is how the British journalists John Micklethwait and Adrian Wooldridge read the mood.

> America's 4,100 universities, whether nominally public or private, are creatures of the market. They relentlessly compete with each other for everything from star faculty to promising students. Most universities are also ruthless money-making machines, forever looking for ways to expand their revenues and maximise their endowments. Academic fees have grown faster than inflation (in 2002 public colleges raised their fees by almost 10 percent). The fact that Harvard is floating on a sea of money does not prevent it from begging its alumni for ever more donations (and giving their children a slight advantage on admissions applications to spur on their generosity).
>
> Students who cannot swim in the university's competitive environment are left to sink. Only half of America's students graduate within five years. The proportion is a mere one in four when you look at students from families with the lowest incomes. When it comes to their professional lives, professors are ruthless practitioners of the economics of inequality. Universities try to improve their position in the academic hierarchy by hiring star professors. And star professors relentlessly try to improve their salaries and perks by flirting with rival institutions.
>
> (Micklethwait and Wooldridge 2005: 371–2)

This no-holds-barred indictment of American universities behaving badly is eerily reminiscent of the attack in Nelson and Watt's *Devil's Dictionary* upon 'corporate universities', universities as 'company towns', and 'superstars' (Nelson and Watt 1999: 78–98, 260–80). Is this indeed the future for the world's most envied system?

To return to the story, *second-order engagement* is generally structured and mediated more by contracts. In this domain the university will produce graduates in required disciplines and professional areas (whether directly or indirectly required to do so). It will respond to perceived needs for particular skills, for professional updating, or to more general consumer demand for courses in particular subjects. It will supply services, research and development, consultancy, and so on, at either a subsidized or a 'for-profit' rate (until recently the university itself often did not know which was which). It may run subsidiary businesses – some as 'spin-outs' or joint ventures, others in the 'service' sector of entertainment, catering, conference or hotel facilities.

Also in this domain the university will often be a very important local and regional economic player. It supplies employment – from unskilled occupations to the very skilled. It provides an expanded consumer base, as students and staff are attracted to the institution and its locality. It offers a steady, well-indemnified customer for goods and services. It is a source of 'development' in a myriad of fields, such as environmental improvements, buildings, amenities, office space, along with some downsides, like controversy over planning, car-parking, congestion or 'studentification'.

'Studentification' is a concept invented by the geographer Darren Smith to capture the issues raised by the social and environmental impact of large numbers of students living in particular areas of a city or town. Smith's chief fieldwork was conducted in Leeds during 2001–02, where he discovered a serious set of problems, and Brighton and Eastbourne, where he did not. The reasons for the difference relate to his major categories of analysis: economic (including effect on house prices and the emergence of houses in multiple occupation – HMO); social (with transient younger people apparently displacing families while establishing their own distinctive 'middle-class' ethos); cultural; and physical. In the former case these conspired to increase tension; in the latter, the communities were apparently both more tolerant and less 'different' than the incomers, who were also more likely to stay. Now UUK has commissioned Smith to produce a 'guide' on how to manage the situation (UUK and SCOP 2006).

The first domain affects the second in some complex and significant ways. Physical *location* is an important element for both the university and its neighbours to understand and respect, with planning consent from local authorities for university developments a litmus test of the state of local relationships.

Meanwhile, the university, as a kind of moral force is expected to behave better than other large organizations (which are similarly concerned about the bottom line).

Some of these cross-over effects are mild: if the university did not pay its bills on time the community would be shocked; if the local hotel did the same thing they would shrug their shoulders. Others are economically more serious. In major partnerships, on which perhaps millions of pounds rest, you will rarely if ever see the university walk away from a done deal. Meanwhile the commercial partner can do so with apparent impunity, citing the business cycle, a change of management or policy, or simply 'market forces'.

*Partnerships* entered into by universities are thereby inherently unequal and in that sense unfair. To say so is not to cry crocodile tears: the university can gain major reputational and practical assets from its first order relationship with the community which, so long as this remains true, can outweigh these downsides. Partnership itself thus throws up some interesting dilemmas, including leading and following (and occasionally having to do both simultaneously). There are also issues about dissolving, renewing and replacing partnership structures and deals, as circumstances change (when this is fudged, the result is often a confusing mixture of new and not-quite-killed-off arrangements, that cause frustration and waste of effort). There is the conflict between moral and strict constructionist views of contracts, as alluded to above. And then there are the expectations of some partnering groups in the community (particularly voluntary and community-service organizations) that the university has been put there (by local or central government) to serve *their* needs. This opens up the issue of relative reputational risk (again as alluded to above), as well as the issue of continuity. Above all, there is the fact that corporate change (mergers, acquisitions and the like) are much less frequent in the university than the corporate (and perhaps even the voluntary sector) – with some notable exceptions.

All of this means that in difficult circumstances the university is likely to be left holding the ring, and should expect to do so. When in early 2006 the Peugeot company announced the closure of its Ryton plant, Ian Marshall, Dean of Engineering and Computing wrote in the *Guardian* that 'Coventry University is the nearest higher education institution ... and we expect to be affected' (Marshall 2006: 10).

A promising way into understanding the dynamics of partnership is through the concept of the *stakeholder*, probably Margaret Thatcher's most influential (and most slippery) legacy to Tony Blair and New Labour. A rigorous 'stakeholder analysis' from the perspective of the university would throw up some surprising results. Questions arise including the following:

- Whose are the stakes on the table (really) in the sense of sharing risk?
- Who can most effectively (that is, legitimately as well as logically) claim to hold the 'third party' stake (the celebrated 'people's money') on behalf of the community as a whole? The politicians would like to claim it is theirs – through democratic validation – although the effect of such violent swings, shifts and reversals of

policy as they employ in public education degrades this trust empirically.

- Is there in fact an inverse ratio of shared risk and rabble-rousing, of nurture and noise? It is clear, for example, that the NHS is one of the system's major stakeholders. It is less clear about the Confederation of British Industry (CBI) or the Institute of Directors (IoD), for example when they are in the mood for general condemnation.

And so, if universities are to make a steady and a positive contribution to their communities, the key holistic concept, and an essential backdrop for questions of leadership and management, has to be the rather old-fashioned notion of *stewardship*, of both the intellectual and moral as well as the concrete and practical assets of the university itself. Who is ultimately responsible for the security, the ongoing contribution and the performance of the university?

The simplest answer to this question is the university itself, through its *governance*. The governing body is straightforwardly responsible for safeguarding the assets (including setting the budget); for setting the strategy (often called 'character and mission'); and for employing and admitting the members (in the case of students through delegation to the Senate or Academic Board) (Shattock 2006: 5–29).

But sometimes these perspectives can be too narrow, especially if they are permanently refracted through the lens of institutional survival. There is a wider social interest in the higher education enterprise (essential to the 'first-order' relationships I set out before), for which governors ought also to feel responsible. This can mean not being too precious (or too competitive) about boundaries, about status, or about the reputational risk of association with other institutions in the sector. *Autonomy* is important, and a source of strength, but it does not apply in a vacuum; it should not be used as an excuse for pushing others around, and it should be used to serve the sector as well as the single institution. In other words, governors too need to understand civic engagement, and how it works.

Who else is responsible for this wider *public interest*? It can be government, although there are dangers there (the university is exactly not the sort of institution to be enlisted in a national crusade). It could be funders (especially through the peculiar agency of the 'buffer body', although genuinely to be one such the body has to be both capable of and seen to be facing both ways). For reasons set out above, it is unlikely to be the less entailed but none the less self-declared 'stakeholders' (the self-interest and the selfish bottom line are just too powerful here). It used to be benefactors (and more generalized well-wishers), and it could be again.

A lot of this relates to the general question of *public confidence.* Does the society have a system of post-compulsory education about which the community feels confident, well served and affectionate? The answer in the UK has to be 'not yet'.

*Third-order engagement* is between the university and its members. Universities are voluntary communities: around the world they are rarely part of the compulsory educational infrastructure of the state (although the state may heavily invest, for its own purposes). Thus they should not be regarded as agents of the state in creating citizens (and certainly not subjects). This is, of course, not to say (following the precepts of 'first-order' relationships) that they do not play a role in ensuring social cohesion, in promoting community solidarity and in problem-solving for policy-makers and practitioners of all kinds.

University members have a similar set of obligations inside the tent; there is also the dimension of *academic citizenship.* To be a full member of a university you have to contribute to more than completing the tasks that happen to be in front of your nose at the time. For traditional academics this has meant collective obligations: to assessment, to committee membership and to strategic scoping; and there is a growing body of literature about such professional academic practice.

What happened in the late twentieth century was the discovery that such practice no longer belonged exclusively to the ranks of the so-called 'faculty'. The teaching, research and service environments are increasingly recognized as being supported and developed by university members with a variety of types of expertise (finance, personnel, estates, libraries, communications and information technology, and so on), each with their own spheres of professional competence, responsibility and recognition.

At the heart of academic citizenship is the concept of *membership.* When you sign up (most obviously as a student, but equally significantly as a staff member), what is the deal? What are the responsibilities that go along with all your rights within the community and, if you are a student, with your entitlements and expectations as a consumer? Such responsibilities include the following:

- a special type of academic honesty, structured most clearly around scientific procedure;
- reciprocity and honesty in expression (for example, by accurately and responsibly referring to other people's work within your own – including to avoid plagiarism);
- academic manners (as in listening to and taking account of other people's views);

- striving towards self-motivation and the capacity for independent learning, along with 'learning how to learn';
- submission to discipline (most clearly in the case of assessment – for both assessors and the assessed);
- respect for the environment in which members of the college or university work; and
- adherence to a set of collectively arrived at commitments and policies (on equalities, grievances, harassment, and so on).

Living according to these values inside the university will profoundly affect how the institution relates to the community outside.

Institutional *strategic choice* and decision-making should ideally come from all of these members of the university community, having of course consulted appropriately outside. But there is a danger here. Universities can too easily become header-tank institutions, doing what is easy rather than what is right.

That said, and to return to the question of autonomy, the evidence is that they make sounder choices when they decide what is right for themselves: when their first-order commitments (who they are) guide their second-order choices (what they do) rather than the other way around. This will be as true of commitments to civic and community engagement as in other spheres of university endeavour. To return to Burton Clark's formulation quoted at the end of Chapter 4, to get what it deserves, a university will have to pass a ten-point test (as summarized below, and in Figure 11.1).

*Figure 11.1* The 'engaged university'

- Course portfolio
- Research
- Community engagement
- A comfortable and enjoyable place to work
- Ethical and environmental responsibility
- Reputation
- Recruitment
- Reflexivity
- Professional contributions
- Surrogacy

It has to devise an attractive, relevant portfolio of courses, and to teach them well. It has to contribute at the highest level in at least some aspects of research. It has to engage with its community, economically and culturally. It has to be a comfortable and enjoyable place to work for everyone: students and staff of all kinds. It has to be, and be seen to be, ethically and environmentally responsible. It has to earn and sustain a positive reputation, locally, nationally and internationally. It has to be able to recruit and to retain good students and good staff. It has to understand itself, where it has come from, what challenges and what opportunities it faces, and how to meet these. It has progressively to play a part in improving the domains in which it works, like education, the environment, or health. Not least, it has to live through its graduates and its external clients, wherever they are and whatever they do.

It is only by operating across this range that a university will meet legitimate expectations for 'first-order', 'second-order' and 'third-order' engagement. In other words, it needs to 'behave well'.

## A twenty-first-century defence of liberal higher education

If there is a slightly recidivist tone to many of these remarks, it is appropriate. Reviewing the historical commitments of universities to their communities, and vice versa, the only truly plausible theoretical model for holding key values together does seem to me to be an updated version of the liberal ideal of higher education.

In July 2001 (the first year of the new century – at least if you follow Queen Victoria's way of counting), I received my copy of a glossy coffee-table book, published by subscription from my undergraduate college. It is called *Clare Through the Twentieth Century*. On the flyleaf it repeats the charge of our Founder in 1359 – Elizabeth de Burgh, Lady Clare – that 'through their study and teaching at the University the scholars should discover and acquire the precious pearl of learning so that it does not stay hidden under a bushel but is displayed abroad to enlighten those who walk in the dark paths of ignorance' (Shaw-Miller 2001). Lady Clare was an early advocate of services to business and the community and 'the third leg'.

My basic argument spans the six and a half centuries between the foundation of Clare College and the present day. As set out in Chapter 2, and put simply, it is that universities have always changed in response to perceived social and economic needs, and they have always remained the same. Also as argued there, the worldly, 'instrumental' side to our business has been matched by an independent, value-laden side. The latter is most eloquently, as well as most practically, expressed through civic and community engagement. What brings these two together is the time-honoured concept of a 'liberal' higher education.

Stanley Katz defines 'liberal education' as 'empowering students, liberating their minds, preparing them for citizenship'. As a *congeries* of aspirations it goes back to Newman, while it received some of its most ambitious formulations in the USA during the last century. However, today, according to Katz, 'liberal education is being asked to carry more freight that it did a century ago, and it is not clear that it can succeed' (Katz 2005: 1). His main target is the 'core curriculum' at Harvard, and his main charges twofold. First, that knowledge has exploded, in all of the disciplines, to the point where 'for undergraduate education, the center simply could not hold'. Secondly, that 'structural changes' in the 'research university' have tended 'to marginalize undergraduate education generally, and more important, make it difficult to theorize and put into effect anything like liberal education' (Katz 2005: 4, 5)

The latest version of the core – the so-called 'approaches to knowledge' template for undergraduate choice of courses – has meanwhile been savagely attacked from the inside (and from the other end of the political spectrum) in Ross Douthat's wonderfully polemical account of his 'accidental' education, *Privilege: Harvard and the Education of the Ruling Class* (Douthat 2005). Douthat's attack is both savage and entertaining. 'Harvard is a terrible mess of a place – an incubator for an American ruling class that is smug, stratified, self-congratulatory, and intellectually adrift.' 'But,' he continues, 'it is a place that I loved' (Douthat 2005: 4). Many of the charges are cultural: 'ours is the privilege that comes with belonging to an upper class grown large enough to fancy itself diverse; fluid and competitive enough to believe itself meritocratic; smart enough for intellectual snobbery but not for intellectual curiosity. Such privilege is wonderfully self-sustaining' (Douthat 2005: 284). However, a vital part of the indictment is educational. Briefly, the core (chose one each from three branches of Literature and Arts, two branches of Historical Studies, Physical Sciences, Life Sciences, Foreign Cultures, Quantitative Reasoning, Moral Reasoning, and Social Analysis), leads to as much of a pot-pourri as close to free choice. 'To separate the trivial from the significant, the wheat from the chaff, is a task for which little guidance is given' (Douthat 2005: 132). Instead, a kind of superficial cleverness is created, together with a highly sophisticated range of ways to evade learning (many of them technological), leading to the unkindest cut of all: 'it was hard work to get into Harvard, and then it was hard work competing [he gives a list of extracurricular examples] . . . But the academics – no, the academics were the easy part' (Douthat 2005: 140).

It may be no accident that in 2005–06 the most popular Harvard course is apparently a class in positive psychology taught by Tal Ben-Shah, the former Israeli national squash champion (with 855 registrations it beats the staple 'Introduction to Economics' which has only 688). (See Ben-Shahar 2006.)

What exactly is going on here? A measured witness is Derek Bok, President of Harvard in the golden era of the 'core' (and recently returned – Red Adair, or at least William Taylor-style) to hold the ring after the brief and eventful tenure of Douthat's hero Larry Summers (2001–06). His latest post-presidential sermon is significantly broader in scope than the Ivy League, the research elite, or even just four-year colleges. The subtitle of *Our Underachieving Colleges* is 'a candid look at how much students learn and why they should be learning more' (Bok 2006). Bok acknowledges, but has ultimately has little sympathy with, the classic American dystopians (led by Allan Bloom), and their arguments that the undergraduate curriculum has lost its purpose; that intellectual standards have been wrecked by political correctness and affirmative action; that instrumentalism has turned universities into 'training grounds for careers'; and that cynical professors now neglect their students. Instead, he is exercised by the prospect of serious international competition for American higher education, and a complacent sense of satisfaction on behalf of both students and graduates.

> a closer look at the record ... shows that colleges and universities, for all of the benefits they bring, accomplish far less for their students than they should. Many seniors graduate without being able to write well enough to satisfy their employers. Many cannot reason clearly or perform competently in analyzing complex, non-technical problems, even though faculties rank critical thinking as the primary goal of a college education. Few undergraduates receiving a degree are able to speak or read a foreign language. Most have never taken a course in quantitative reasoning or acquired the knowledge needed to be a reasonably informed citizen in a democracy. And these are only some of the problems.
>
> (Bok 2006: 1–8)

The latest twist in the story is yet another proposal (in October 2006) to revamp the core; this time from a group led by Louis Menand, Professor of English and American Literature and Language, and a sometime cheer-leader for the dystopian tendency elaborated in Chapter 9 (see Menand 2001). The new framework requires one course from each of seven branches (characterized as 'exposures to major arenas of change and influence in the 21st century': Reason and Faith; the Ethical Life; Cultural Traditions and Cultural Change; the United States – Historical and Global Perspectives; Societies of the

World – Historical and Global Perspectives; Life Science; and Physical Science. It is the first that has attracted the most attention; perhaps it is returning Harvard to its roots; perhaps it is a reflection that the Enlightenment project of the university may not be enough to respond to the contemporary world. Menand is quoted as follows: 'twenty years ago we may not have thought it was that important that students need to understand something about religion, but we felt that it is something secular universities may not be preparing students to deal with' (Wilson, R. 2006).

Why does this matter? It matters partly because, at least in the American system, in the words of Donald Kagan, former Dean of Yale, 'as goes Harvard ... ' (Kagan 2006). It also matters because it reflects the drive, and the anxiety, within the academy to get these things right. If one of the theses of this book is correct, they will never be exactly right, but the striving is essential. Bok's main complaint – apparently swiftly responded to by at least some of his rediscovered colleagues – seems to be that the 'core' is not working; that the 'inner game' set out in Chapter 9 has failed. However, my contention, in that chapter and here, is that other things are going on, which should cause us to be significantly more optimistic about the prospects of further renewal of the university enterprise. Many of these relate to the contemporary management of civic and community engagement. Debates such as this are critical to the social role of higher education, notably through 'first-order' engagement.

Bringing the argument back to the UK, I would like to conclude by commenting on ten current misunderstandings (as I see them) about universities and the prospects for survival and prosperity of liberal higher educational values. In the 'propositions' which follow, I seek to apply the injunctions of both Figure 9.6 (the higher education 'commandments') and 11.1 (the 'engaged university').

Proposition one: *there can be no 'academic freedom' without what Donald Kennedy (former President of Stanford) calls 'academic duty'* (Kennedy 1997). Academics are now more regularly (and more intensively) required to explain what they are up to and why it is important. They can (and the best of them do) make a virtue of engagement in a wider series of 'conversations', inside and outside the academy. Nothing here should inhibit the pursuit of difficult ideas wherever they may lead. A common, if occasionally pompous, expression of this intention is the commitment of members of the university to be 'public intellectuals'.

Proposition two: *these values apply across the curriculum.* Arguments, for example, that they belong exclusively either to science or the humanities (and not to the other) are naive and usually allied to arguments for resources (for example, Save British Science, or the lengthy campaign that led to an Arts and Humanities Research Council). By my account they are both historically insensitive and epistemologically indefensible.

Proposition three: *they apply equally to professional and/or vocational courses.* The discussions of 'capital' in Chapter 2 are particularly relevant here, and especially the dangers of a narrowly instrumental view of what graduates as employees as well as citizens can expect to take from their experience. I have tried to demonstrate how it can diminish the moral and social as well as the economic contribution of higher education.

Proposition four: *liberal values permeate mode 2 knowledge creation and use, at least as much as they were present in mode 1* (see Figure 9.3). The third 'misunderstanding' leads to a fourth, almost a corollary: that liberal values exist independent of (and indeed can be corrupted by) 'real-world' dilemmas. It is, of course, in aspects of professional practice that values are either socially embedded or ignored.

Proposition five: *the entire higher education sector is involved.* Perhaps most dangerous is the anti-democratic notion that higher education liberal values belong predominantly to an exclusive (or elite) group of institutions. Again, I have a suspicion of academic and institutional foul play in this argument. It allies a pre-emptive strike for resources with social snobbery.

Proposition six: *liberal values lie at the heart of an HEI's connection with its communities.* It is just not true that such values are incapable of lay expression or adoption. The case for a 'wider conversation' has been powerfully extended by the ACU's concept of 'engagement as a core value for the university', with which this book began. This issues into a conviction that 'universities need to be part of the conscience of democratic society and students helped to gain skills not just for their working life but also to participate as citizens' (ACU 2002: i).

Proposition seven: *'keeping the faith' in this way is hard work and requires constant attention.* I have tried to argue that liberal values in HE have a mixed status in practice: some are relatively secure; some are in urgent need of restoration, and some have to be specifically reconstructed to meet new demands.

Proposition eight: *in preserving liberal values we must guard against the kind of proxy battles described by Gordon Graham (above).* In particular, it is an easy populist target to suggest that they will be corroded by either interventionist public policy or by effective internal 'management'. Again, I have tried to counteract some of the more apocalyptic accounts of what is going on. There is no reason why funders (including the representatives of the state) and leaders (of institutions, of departments, and of groups) should not be able to operate 'with the grain' of liberal commitments. Indeed, I suggest that it is in their interests to do so.

Proposition nine: *lifelong learning is key* (Eliot *et al.* 1996; Watson and Taylor 1998). It is an easy, but false, assumption to suggest that students and staff leave these ways of thinking behind when they move on (see the discussion of the Oakeshottian 'gift of an interval' in Chapter 9). The ACU document has an attractive formula to challenge this assumption. It suggests that 'the best academic qualifications might be more like membership of a club of those pledged to return to study at intervals in the future' (ACU 2002: 20).

Proposition ten: *to echo the final 'commandment', we should indeed never be satisfied*. Last but not least, there are dangers in believing anybody who tries to tell us definitively what liberal higher education values are. The university of 2050 will be just as different from that of 2000 as that of 1950, or even 1350. I do, however, have a suspicion that Lady Clare's commitment to a context-specific type of civic and community engagement will still be relevant.

# REFERENCES

Ahier, J., Beck, J. and Moore, R. (2002) *Graduate Citizens? Issues of Citizenship and Higher Education*. London: Routledge Falmer.

Altbach, P. (2004) The costs and benefits of world-class universities, *Academe*, (June): 1–5.

Appiah, K.A. (2006) *Cosmopolitanism: Ethics in a World of Strangers*. London: Allen Lane.

Arthur, J. with Bohlin, K.E. (eds) (2005) *Citizenship and Higher Education: The Role of Universities in Communities and Societies*. London: Routledge Falmer.

Ashby, E. (1959) *Technology and the Academics*. London: Macmillan.

Ashby, E. (1969) A Hippocratic oath for the academic profession, *Minerva*, 8(1): 64–6.

Ashton, L. (2003) *Higher Education Supply and Demand to 2010*. Oxford: HEPI.

Association of Commonwealth Universities (ACU) (2002) *Engagement as a Core Value for the University: A Consultation Document*. London: ACU.

Baker, R. (2006) Talking it up, *New York Review of Books*, 11 May: 4–6.

Barham, N. (2004) *Disconnected: Why our Kids Are Turning their Backs on Everything We Thought We Knew*. London: Random House.

Bell, D.A. (2006) Teaching political theory in Beijing, *Dissent*, Spring. www.dissentmagazine.org/issue/?issues=38 (31 Oct. 2006).

Ben-Shahar, T. (2006) Make lemonade out of lemons, *Education Guardian*, 25 April.

Benneworth, P.S. and Dawley, S.J. (2006) Managing the university third strand innovation process: developing innovation support services in regionally engaged universities, *Knowledge, Technology and Policy*, 18(3): 74–94.

Bloom, A. (1998) *The Closing of the American Mind*. New York: Simon and Schuster.

Blumenstyk, G. (2006) U. of Phoenix buys naming rights to a pro-football stadium, *Chronicle of Higher Education*, 27 September.

Blunkett, D. (2000) *Modernising Higher Education: Facing the Global Challenge*. Speech at the University of Greenwich, 15 February. London: DfEE.

Bok, D. (2006) *Our Underachieving Colleges: A Candid Look at How Much Students Learn and Why They Should Be Learning More.* Princeton, NJ, and Oxford: Princeton University Press.

Bowen, W.G., Kurzweilk, M.A. and Tobin, E.M. (2005) *Equity and Excellence in American Higher Education.* Charlottesville, VA: University of Virginia Press.

Boyer, P.J. (2006) Big men on campus: the lacrosse furor and Duke's divided culture, *The New Yorker*, 4 September: 44–61.

Brennan, J., King, R. and Lebeau, J. (2004) *The Role of Universities in the Transformation of Societies: An International Research Project (Synthesis Report).* London: Centre for Higher Education Research and Information.

Broers, A. (2005) University courses for tomorrow, 3rd HEPI Annual Lecture, The Royal Institution, November.

Brown, L. and Muirhead, B. (2001) The civic mission of Australian universities, *Engaged Perspectives* (University of Queensland), July.

Brown, N., Corney, M. and Stanton, G. (2004) *Breaking Out of the Silos: 14–30 Education and Skills Policy.* London: Nigel Brown Associates.

Brown, R. and Ternmouth, P. (2006) *International Competitiveness: Businesses Working with UK Universities.* London: CIHE.

Browning, G. (2004) How to be fair, *The Guardian*, 18 September.

Bynner, J., Dolton, P., Feinstein L., Makepiece, G., Malmberg, L. and Woods, L. (2003) *Revisiting the Benefits of Higher Education: A Report by the Bedford Group for Lifecourse and Statistical Studies, Institute of Education.* Bristol: HEFCE.

Clark, B.R. (2004) *Sustaining Change in Universities: Continuities in Case Studies and Concepts.* Maidenhead: SRHE and Open University Press.

Committee of Vice-Chancellors and Principals (CVCP) (1995) *Public Expenditure Survey Submission 1995: The Case for Increased Investment in Universities.* London: CVCP.

Community University Partnership Programme (CUPP) (2006) *CUPP Conference Report.* University of Brighton (April). www.cupp.org.uk/conference.htm (31 Oct. 2006).

Côté, J. (2002) The role of identity capital in the transition to adulthood: the individualization thesis examined, *Journal of Youth Studies*, 5(2): 117–34.

Council for Industry and Higher Education (CIHE) (2002) *Recruiting from a Wider Spectrum of Graduates.* London: CIHE.

Curtis, P. (2005) Minds wide open, *The Guardian*, 15 February.

Delanty, G. (2001) *Challenging Knowledge: The University in the Knowledge Society.* Buckingham: SRHE and Open University Press.

Department for Education and Employment (DfEE) (1998) *The Learning Age: A Renaissance for a New Britain.* London: HMSO.

Department for Education and Skills (DfES) (2003) *The Future of Higher Education*, White Paper, Cmnd 5735. Norwich: The Stationery Office.

Department for Education and Skills (DfES) (2004a) *Fair Admissions to Higher Education: Draft Recommendations for Consultation.* London: DfES.

Department for Education and Skills (DfES) (2004b) *Fair Admissions to Higher Education: Recommendations for Good Practice.* London: DfES.

Department for Education and Skills (DfES) (2004c) *Putting the World into World-class Education.* London: DfES.

Department for Education and Skills (DfES) (2006) *FE Reform White Paper: Raising Skills, Improving Life Chances*. London: DfES.

Douthat, G.R. (2005) *Privilege: Harvard and the Education of the Ruling Class*. New York: Hyperion.

Duan, Xin-Ran (2003) Chinese higher education enters a new era, *Academe*. www.aaup.org/publications/Academe/2003/03nd/03ndduanhtm (31 Oct. 2006).

Duke, C. (2003) University engagement and the traditions of the Universities Association for Continuing Education – what next future? Presentation for the UACE Annual Conference, Building Bridges, University of Newcastle, 14–16 April. Mimeo.

Edwards, M. (2004) *Civil Society*. Cambridge: Polity.

Elliot, J., Francis, H., Humphreys, R. and Istance, R. (eds) (1996) *Communities and their Universities: The Challenge of Lifelong Learning*. London: Lawrence and Wishart.

European University Association (EUA)/American Council on Education (ACE) (2004) *Charting the Course between Public Service and Commercialisation: Prices Values and Quality*. Turin: Conference proceedings, 3–5 June.

Evans, K. (2003) Learning for a living? The powerful, the dispossessed, and the learning revolution, University of London, Institute of Education professorial lecture, 19 February.

Evans, M. (2004) *Killing Thinking: The Death of the Universities*. London and New York: Continuum.

Fain, P. (2005a) Penn seen as a model for community partnerships, *Chronicle of Higher Education*, 22 July.

Fain, P. (2005b) Tufts Will Use $100-million gift to make profitable 'microloans' in developing world, *Chronicle of Higher Education*, 11 November.

Fitzgerald, F. (2005) Peculiar institutions: Brown University looks at the slave traders in its past, *The New Yorker*, 12 September: 68–77.

Florida, R. (2002) *The Rise of the Creative Class, and How It's Transforming Work Leisure, Community and Creative Life*. New York: Basic Books.

Florida, R. (2005) *The Flight of the Creative Class: The New Global Competition for Talent*. New York: HarperBusiness.

Foxwood, H. (ed.) (2006) *Higher Education: Seminars Held between March and July 2003*. London: The Smith Institute.

Frand, J.L. (2000) The information age mindset; changes in students and implications for higher education, *Educause Review*, 35(5): 14–24.

Freeman, M. (2004) Educational settlements, in *The Encyclopedia of Informal Education*. www.ifed.org/association/educational_settlements_htm (accessed 31 Oct. 2006).

Further Education Funding Council (FEFC) (1997) *Learning Works* (Kennedy Report). Coventry: FEFC.

Gallwey, W.T. (1975) *The Inner Game of Tennis*. London: Jonathan Cape.

Gibbons, M., Limoges, C., Nowotny, H., Schwarzman, S., Scott, P. and Trow, M. (1994) *The New Production of Knowledge: The Dynamics of Science and Research in Contemporary Societies*. London: Sage.

Gittleman, S. (2004) *The Entrepreneurial University: The Transformation of Tufts, 1976–2002*. Hanover: University of New England Press.

Gorard, S., Smith, E., May, H., Thomas, L., Adnett, N. and Slack, K. (2006) *Review of Widening Participation Research: Addressing the Barriers to Participation in Higher Education*. HEFCE. www.hefce.ac.uk/pubs/rdreports/2006/rd13_06/ (accessed 31 Oct. 2006).

Gourley, B. (2006) A declaration of independence, *Commonwealth* (with *Times Higher Educational Supplement*) 31 March: 4–5.

Graham, G. (2005), *The Institution of Intellectual Values: Realism and Idealism in Higher Education*. Charlottesville, VA: Imprint Academic.

Gray, J. (2006) The global delusion, *New York Review of Books*, 27 April: 20–3.

Guttman, A. (1987) *Democratic Education*. Princeton, NJ: Princeton University Press.

Harkavy, I. and Benson, L. (1998) De-platonizing and democratizing education as the basis of service learning, in R. Rhoades (ed.) *Academic Service-Learning: A Pedagogy of Action and Reflection*. San Francisco, CA: Jossey-Bass.

Hart, A. and Wolff, D. (2006) Developing local 'communities of practice' through local community–university partnerships. *Planning, Practice & Research*, 21(1): 121–38.

Harvey, L. (1999) The sense in satisfaction, *Times Higher Education Supplement*, 15 January: 29.

Her Majesty's Treasury (HMT), Department of Trade and Industry (DTI) and Department for Education and Skills (DfES) (2004) *Science & Innovation Investment Framework 2004–2014*. London: The Stationery Office.

Higher Education Funding Council for England (HEFCE) (2003) *Joint Consultation on the Review of Research Assessment*. (Roberts Review.) Bristol: HEFCE.

Higher Education Funding Council for England (HEFCE) (2004) *Terms of Reference for Working Group to Derive Third Stream Social, Civic and Cultural Indicators*. Bristol: HEFCE.

Higher Education Funding Council for England (HEFCE) (2005) *Higher Education Innovation Fund Round 3: Invitation and Guidance for Institutional Plans and Competitive Bids*. Invitation 2005/46, Bristol: HEFCE.

Higher Education Funding Council for England (HEFCE) (2006) *Strategic Plan, 2006–11*. Guide 2006/13, Bristol: HEFCE.

Higher Education Policy Institute (HEPI) (2004a) *Projecting Demand for UK Higher Education from the Accession Countries*. HEPI Report Summary 8. Oxford: HEPI.

Higher Education Policy Institute (HEPI) (2004b), *Credit Accumulation and Transfer and the Bologna Process: An Overview*. HEPI: Oxford.

Higher Education Policy Institute (HEPI) (2006) *How Exposed are English Universities to Reductions in Demand from International Students?* Oxford: HEPI.

Higher Education Statistics Agency (HESA) (2004/05), *Reference Volume: Resources in Higher Education*. London: HESA.

Iacobucci, F. and Tuohy, C. (eds) (2005) *Taking Public Universities Seriously*. Toronto: University of Toronto Press.

Institute of Business Ethics (IBE) and Council for Industry and Higher Education (CIHE) (2005) *Ethics Matters: Managing Ethical Issues in Higher Education*. London: CIHE.

Jackson, S., Ajayi, S. and Quigley, M. (2005) *Going to University from Care.* London: Institute of Education.

James, W. (1981) *The Principles of Psychology.* Cambridge, MA: Harvard University Press. First published 1890.

Jessop, S.K. (2006) Have foreign MBA, will travel in Chinese business, *International Herald Tribune*, 14 February: 17.

Jones, R.A. (2005) Where the boys aren't, *Crosstalk*, 13(12), www.higher-education.org/crosstalk/ct0205/news0205-boys.shtml (31 Oct. 2006).

Kagan, D. (2006) As goes Harvard ... , *Commentary*, 22 September.

Kanter, R.M. (1995) *World Class: Thriving Locally in the Global Economy.* New York: Simon and Schuster.

Katz, S. (2005) Liberal education on the ropes, *Chronicle of Higher Education*, 1 April.

Kay, J. (2003) *The Truth about Markets: Their Genius, their Limits, their Follies.* London: Allen Lane.

Kennedy, D. (1997) *Academic Duty.* Cambridge, MA, and London: Harvard University Press.

Kirp, D. (2005) Stanford of the Northwest, *Crosstalk*, 13(1): 13–14.

Labi, A. (2006) Germany awards 'elite' status and extra funds to 3 universities, *Chronicle of Higher Education*, 16 October.

Lambert, R. (2003) *Lambert Review of Business–University Collaboration.* Norwich: HMSO.

Lang, D.W. (2005) 'World class' or the curse of comparison, *Canadian Journal of Higher Education*, 35(3): 27–55.

Lay, S. (2004) *The Interpretation of the Magna Charta Universitatum and its Principles.* Bologna: Bononia University Press.

Macfarlane, B. (2005) *Teaching with Integrity: The Ethics of Higher Education Practice.* London: Routledge Falmer.

MacLeod, D. and Curtis, P. (2004) All you need is students, *The Guardian*, 17 February.

Marshall, I. (2006) Peugeot quits, but universities are there for the long haul, *Education Guardian*, 25 April.

Marginson, S. (1997) *Educating Australia: Government, Economy and Citizen since 1960.* Melbourne: Cambridge University Press.

Maurrasse, D.J. (2001) *Beyond the Campus: How Colleges and Universities Form Partnerships with their Communities.* New York and London: Routledge.

May, Lord R. (2004) *Global Problems and Global Science: Anniversary Address 2004.* London: The Royal Society.

Menand, L. (2001) College: the end of a golden era, *New York Review of Books*, 18 October: 44–7.

Menand, L. (2006) Name that tone. *The New Yorker*, 26 June: 21–2.

Micklethwait, J. and Wooldridge, A. (2005) *The Right Nation: Why America Is Different.* London: Penguin Books.

Miller, S. (2006) *Conversation: A History of a Declining Art.* New Haven, CT, and London: Yale University Press.

Mount, F. (2004) *Mind the Gap: The New Class Divide in Britain.* London: Short Books.

Musil, C.T. (2003) Education for citizenship, *Peer Review*, 5(3): 4–8.

National Commission on Education (NCE) (2003) *Learning to Succeed: The Next Decade*. Brighton: University of Brighton Education Research Centre.

National Committee of Inquiry into Higher Education (NCIHE) (1997) *Higher Education in the Learning Society* (Dearing Report). London: HMSO.

Nelson, C. and Watt, S. (1999) *Academic Keywords: A Devil's Dictionary for Higher Education*. New York and London: Routledge.

Nixon, J. (2004) Education for the good society: the integrity of academic practice, *London Review of Education*, 2(3): 245–52.

Nussbaum, M.C. (2002) Education for citizenship in a era of global connection, *Studies in Philosophy and Education*, 21(4–5): 289–303.

O'Leary, J. (2006), Developing countries 'cannot reverse brain drain', ACU told. *Times Higher Education Supplement*, 21 April.

Ostrander, S. (2006) Civic engagement as a Tufts signature: lessons from five schools. http://uccps.tufts.edu/05_Faculty/OstranderSummary.html (accessed 31 Oct. 2006).

Pan, Su-Yan (2006) Economic globalization, politico-cultural identity and university autonomy; the struggle of Tsinghua University in China, *Journal of Education Policy*, 21(3): 245–66.

Pemberton, S. and Winn, S. (2005) *The Financial Situation of Students at the University of Brighton: The Fourteenth Report, 2004/05*. Health and Social Policy Research Centre, University of Brighton.

Public and Corporate Economic Consultants (PACEC) (2004) *Economic and Social Impact of the University of Hertfordshire on Welwyn Hatfield*. Cambridge and London: PACEC.

Reich, R. (2004) *The Destruction of Public Higher Education in America, and How the UK Can Avoid the Same Fate*. 2nd annual HEPI lecture, 25 March. Oxford: HEPI.

Rhodes, F.H.T. (2001) *The Creation of the Future: the role of the American university*. Ithaca and London: Cornell U. Press.

Robinson, S. and Katalushi, C. (eds) (2005) *Values in Higher Education*. Castle-upon-Alum: Aureus and the University of Leeds.

Schuller, T. (1998) Social capital and community-building, in K. Hurley (ed.) *University Continuing Education in Partnership for Development, UACE Annual Conference 1997, Proceedings*. Leeds: UACE.

Schuller, T., Preston, J., Hammond, C., Brassett-Grundy, A. and Bynner, J. (2004) *The Benefits of Learning: The Impact of Education on Health, Family Life and Social Capital*. London: Routledge Falmer.

Scott, P. (1995) *The Meanings of Mass Higher Education*. Buckingham: SRHE and Open University Press.

Sennett, R. (2003) *Respect: The Formation of Character in an Age of Inequality*. London: Allen Lane.

Sennett, R. (2006) *The Culture of the New Capitalism*. New Haven, CT, and London: Yale University Press.

Shattock, M. (2006) *Managing Good Governance*. Maidenhead: Open University Press.

Shaw-Miller, L. (ed.) (2001), *Clare Through the Twentieth Century*. Lingfield, Surrey: Third Millennium.

Showalter, E. (2005) *Faculty Towers: The Academic Novel and its Discontents* Oxford: Oxford University Press.

Silver, H. (2003) *Higher Education and Opinion-Making in Twentieth Century England*. London and Portland, OR: Frank Cass.

Skidelsky, R. (2006) Truck and barter (review of Erik Ringmar, *Surviving Capitalism: how we learned to live with market and remained almost human*), *New Statesman*, 24 April: 55–6.

Slowey, M. and Watson, D. (2003) *Higher Education and the Lifecourse*. Maidenhead: SRHE and Open University Press.

Smith, C. (2005) Understanding trust and confidence: two paradigms and their significance for health and social care, *Journal of Applied Philosophy*, 22(3): 299–316.

Social and Organisational Mediation of University Learning (SOMUL) (2005) *Working Paper 2*. SOMUL: York.

Stella, A. and Woodhouse, D. (2006) Ranking of higher education institutions. Melbourne, AUQA. Mimeo.

Stevens, R. (2004) *University to Uni: The Politics of Higher Education in England since 1944*. London: Politico's.

Sunderland, N., Muirhead, B., Parsons, R. and Holtom, D. (2004) *The Australian Consortium on Higher Education, Community Engagement and Social Responsibility*. University of Queensland: Boilerhouse Centre.

Talloires (Talloires Conference on the Civic Roles and Social Responsibilities of Higher Education) (2005) *Strengthening the Civic Roles and Social Responsibilities of Higher Education: Building a Global Network*. Tufts University. www.tufts.edu/talloiresnetwork/TalloiresDeclaration2005.pdf. (accessed 18 Dec. 2006).

Thirunamachandran, R. (2006) The impact of research and knowledge transfer policy on UKHE, presentation at University of Kyoto, 2 February, Mimeo.

Tomorrow Group (2005) *Working in the Twenty-First Century*. London: ESRC and the Tomorrow Group.

UNITE (2005) The UNITE student experience report 2005. www.mori.com/polls/2004/unite-jan.shtml (accessed 31 Oct. 2006).

Universities UK (UUK) (2003) Information for members – 'Secretary of State's grant letter to HEFCE on funding and delivery to 2005–06', 23 January.

Universities UK (UUK) (2004a) *Participating and Performing: Sport and Higher Education in the UK*. London: UUK.

Universities UK (UUK) (2004b) Putting the HE into health – universities, health and social care, note from the UUK Longer Term Strategy Group and the Health Committee joint seminar, April.

Universities UK (UUK) (2005) *Patterns of Higher Education Institutions in the UK: Fifth Report*. London: UUK.

Universities UK (UUK) (2006a) The future student experience, report of a seminar of the UUK Longer Term Strategy and Student Experience Groups, March.

Universities UK (UUK) (2006b) *Patterns of Higher Education Institutions in the UK: Sixth Report*. London: UUK.

Universities UK (UUK) and Standing Committee of Principals (SCOP) (2006) *Studentification: A Guide to Opportunities, Challenges and Practices*. London: UUK.

University of Cambridge (2004) *Community Engagement Report, 2003–4: A Report on the University of Cambridge's Outreach Activities*. Cambridge: University of Cambridge.

Van Der Werf, M. (2006) Brown U. acknowledges its founders' ties to slavery but stops short of apologizing. *Chronicle of Higher Education*, 19 October.

Watson, D. (2000), *Managing Strategy*. Buckingham: Open University Press.

Watson, D. (2002) Can we all do it all? Tensions in the structure and mission of UK higher education, *Higher Education Quarterly*, 56(2): 143–55.

Watson, D. (2003) *Universities and Civic Engagement: A Critique and a Prospectus.* www.uq.edu.au/insideout/proceed.htm (accessed 31 Oct. 2006).

Watson, D. (2005a) Will lifelong learning networks work? A perspective from higher education, *Journal of Access Policy and Practice*, 2(2): 187–205.

Watson, D. (2005b) What I think I know and don't know about widening participation in HE, in C. Duke and G. Layer (eds) *Widening Participation: Which Way Forward for English Higher Education?* Leicester: NIACE.

Watson, D. (2006) UK HE: the truth about the market, *Higher Education Review*, 38(3): 3–16.

Watson, D. and Bowden, R. (2000) *After Dearing: A Mid-term Report*, University of Brighton Education Research Centre Occasional Paper, University of Brighton, July.

Watson, D. and Bowden, R. (2002) *The New University Decade, 1992–2002*, University of Brighton Education Research Centre Occasional Paper, University of Brighton, September.

Watson, D. and Bowden, R. (2005) *The Turtle and the Fruit Fly: New Labour and UK Higher Education, 2001–2005*, University of Brighton Education Research Centre Occasional Paper, University of Brighton, May.

Watson, D. and Maddison, E. (2005) *Managing Institutional Self-Study*. Maidenhead: Open University Press.

Watson, D. and Taylor, R. (1998) *Lifelong Learning and the University: A Post-Dearing Agenda*. London: Falmer Press.

Wedgwood, M. (2003) Making engagement work in practice, in S. Bjarnsson and P. Coldstream (eds) *The Idea of Engagement: Universities in Society*. London: Association of Commonwealth Universities.

Wedgwood, M. (2006) Mainstreaming the third stream, in I. McNay (ed.) *Beyond Mass Higher Education: Building on Expansion*. Maidenhead: Open University Press.

Weeks, J. (2006) Civic and community engagement: the University of Pennsylvania and beyond, presentation to CUPP conference, University of Brighton, 6 April. Mimeo.

Wickenden, D. (2006) Top of the class. *The New Yorker*, 2 October: 35–6.

Wilde, S., Wright, S., Hayward, G., Johnson, J. and Skerret, R. (2006) *Nuffield Review Higher Education Focus Groups: Preliminary Report*. Oxford: Nuffield Review of 14–19 Education & Training.

Williams, G. (2006) 'Infrastructures of responsibility': the moral tasks of institutions, *Journal of Applied Philosophy*, 23(2): 207–21.

Wilson, A. (2006) From ivory tower to sporting cathedral, *The Guardian*, 6 April.

Wilson, P. (2006) Gaining friends and encouraging participation: a summary of the University of Cambridge's community engagement survey, *Ad Lib: Journal for Continuing Liberal Adult Education*, 31(September): 6–8.

Wilson, R. (2006) New plan to overhaul Harvard curriculum singles out religion and American history for study. *Chronicle of Higher Education*, 10 October.

Winter, A., Wiseman, J. and Muirhead, B. (forthcoming) University–community engagement in Australia: practice, policy and public good, *Education, Citizenship and Social Justice*.

Wolf, A. (2003) *Does Education Matter? Myths about Education and Economic Growth*. London: Penguin.

Wolf, A. (2006) Opinion, *Times Higher Education Supplement*, 21 April.

Wolfe, T. (2004) *I Am Charlotte Simmons: A Novel*. London: Jonathan Cape.

Zhou Ji (2006) *Higher Education in China*. Singapore: Thomson Learning.

# LIST OF WEBSITES

(All last accessed on 31 October 2006 unless stated otherwise.)

*Australia*
Australian Universities Community Engagement Alliance Inc. (AUCEA) – www.aucea.net.au
University of Queensland Boilerhouse Community Engagement Centre – www.uq.edu.au/boilerhouse/
Department of Education, Science and Training, Learning and Teaching Performance Fund – www.dest.gov.au/sectors/higher_education/policy_ issues_reviews/key_issues/learning_teaching/ltpf/

*UK*
Community–University Partnership Programme – www.cupp.org.uk
Higher Education Active Community Fund – http://www.hefce.ac.uk/reach-out/heacf/
National Committee of Inquiry into Higher Education (Dearing Committee) – http://www.leeds.ac.uk/educol/ncihe/
The Nuffield Foundation – www.nuffieldfoundation.org/
Social and Organisational Mediation of University Learning project – www.open.ac.uk/cheri/SOMULhome.htm
Teaching and Learning Research Programme – www.tlrp.org
University of Bristol, Centre for Public Engagement – www.bris.ac.uk/cms/cpe
University of Sheffield Charter – www.shef.ac.uk/calendar/incorp.html (accessed 19 Dec. 2006)

*USA*
American Association of Colleges & Universities Center for Liberal Education and Civic Engagement – www.aacu.org/civic_engagement
Campus Compact – http://www.compact.org/
Center for Community Partnerships – http://www.upenn.edu/ccp/index.shtml

Innovations in Civic Participation – www.icip.org/
University of Minnesota Council on Public Engagement – www.engagement.umn.edu/cope/reports/appendices02.html (accessed 20 Dec. 2006)

*International*
Association of Commonwealth Universities – http://www.acu.ac.uk/engagement
Council of Europe Forum on Higher Education and Democratic Culture – http://dc.ecml.at
Essential Science Indicators – www.isinet.com/
G-Factor – www.universitymetrics.com/g-factor
International Consortium for Higher Education, Civic Responsibility and Democracy – http://iche.sas.upenn.edu/index/index.htm
Shanghai Jaio Tong 'top 500 universities' – http://ed.sjtu.edu.cn/ranking.htm
Social Science Research Network – http://ssrn.com
Talloires Declaration – www.tufts.edu/talloiresnetwork/TalloiresDeclaration2005.pdf (accessed 18 Dec. 2006)
*THES* world ranking of universities – www.thes.co.uk/worldrankings/
Universitas 21 – www.universitas21.com/memberlist.html
Webometrics – http://www.webometrics.info/

# INDEX